Volume 22, Number 1, March 2007                    Issue 50

# Focus on Queer Postcolonial

## Articles

## Reviews

# 'Our people know the difference, black is a race, jew is a religion, f*g**tism is a sin'

## Towards a Queer Postcolonial Hermeneutics

The idea for this special issue occurred to me in 2004, at a time when the violent anti-gay content of a number of Jamaican dancehall lyrics became a focus of critical attention for concerned members of lesbian, gay, bisexual, transgendered, queer (LGBTQ) and human rights communities in Jamaica, the USA and the UK. During heated debates in the media and the courts, what looked like the expression of homosexual panic by Jamaican deejays and their supporters was countered by a form of 'border panic' (Harper et al 1), in which performers were stopped and questioned at London's Heathrow airport, placed under close police and legal scrutiny, and in some cases prevented from performing in British, Canadian and US venues (Sizzla was banned from entering the UK in November 2004, and Beenie Man, Buju Banton, Elephant Man, Vybz Kartel, TOK, Capleton and Bounty Killer were investigated by Scotland Yard).[1] The arguments and debates surrounding the lyrics, the court orders and the police investigations into the so-called 'dancehall eight' (Oumano) were emotional and mutually accusatory, and I found myself struggling to envisage what sort of discursive ethical ground could be occupied (however tentatively) by theorists in the emerging field of queer postcolonial studies, in order to begin to comprehend and critique this seemingly intractable nexus of sex, sexuality, gender, race, nationality, class and religion. What does it mean to be postcolonially queer, or/and queerly postcolonial, particularly in a context where the self-styled 'local' values of the post-colony are pitted against what are regarded as the permissive sexual mores of the west? Are diaspora and transnational identities *inevitably* queer in their border-crossings, their lability, their destabilising mobility and multiplicity? If this is the case, why has 'queer' seemed marginal to postcolonial discourse until quite recently?

A number of texts have begun to map out this troubled, troubling, but important terrain: among them, the special issues of *Social Text* and *ARIEL* which appeared in 1997 and 1999 respectively; collections such as Patton and Sánchez-Eppler's *Queer Diasporas* (2000), John C Hawley's *Postcolonial, Queer* (2001), Johnson and Henderson's *Black Queer Studies* (2005); and studies by (among others), Gayatri Gopinath, José Esteban Muñoz and Siobhan B Somerville.[2] All the same, in spite of the increasing number of published materials which deal with the 'queer transexions of race, nation, [sexuality] and gender' (to cite the *Social Text* special issue), it still seems to be the case that the junction of race and sexuality is a discursive locale that many people would prefer to avoid (Dollimore 332).

Such evasiveness did not characterise the events of 2004, when LGBTQ activists were tireless in their efforts to track and censure/censor dancehall deejays, and a number of Jamaican commentators were equally vociferous in response to what was widely regarded as Western interventionism. The claim that Jamaica was one of the world's most homophobic societies was dismissed as spurious and unfounded; any violence expressed in the songs was metaphorical, 'lyrical' even; and it was argued that the connection between such expressions and *physical* violence was tenuous, since there was no hard evidence that dancehall fans ever went out and murdered gay people as a result of listening to the offending songs. Indeed, for many, this was a clear-cut case of neo-colonialism: not only had the lyrics been de-contextualised, mistranslated and misunderstood by non-Jamaicans, but human rights campaigners had no business telling Jamaicans what to do.[3] Writing in the *Jamaica Gleaner*, Donna Hope

*Wasafiri Vol. 22, No. 1 March 2007, pp. 1–5*

ISSN 0269-0055 print/ISSN 1747-1508 online © 2007 Wasafiri
http://www.tandf.co.uk/journals    DOI: 10.1080/02690050601097534

insisted that although Jamaica's constitutional criminalisation of sex between men should certainly be 'expunged as a matter of urgency', such reform

> should not be as a result of pressure from gay or human rights groups, led by white foreigners who feel that it is time for 'those black people in Jamaica to get with the programme'; but rather as a part of a Jamaican thrust to provide a level playing field for all its citizens, regardless of sexual preference. ('Clash')

A blogger in the *Jamaica Star* put the case in far harsher terms: objecting to Peter Tatchell's contention that the organisers of the MOBO (Music of Black Origin) Awards were 'colluding with artists who encourage the killing of queers', and that 'the Mobos would never accept the nomination of a singer who incited the gassing of Jewish people' (Wilson), the *Star* blogger urged '[a]ll true Jamaicans [to] stand up and support our values [at] home or abroad . . . Our people are not stupid,' continued the blogger:

> what the hell was peter (gay leader guy) saying when he gave example of people singing against black or Jew saying it is the same thing, it called racism. ** Our people know the difference, black is a race, jew [*sic*] is a religion, f*g**tism [*sic*] is a sin. How can this punk class gay as race. ('Reggae activist needed')

I have chosen to focus on this particular ideological node not because I think it is unique to Jamaica, but because of its exemplary, multi-layered complexity, notwithstanding the *Star* blogger's enraged attempt to simplify 'race', 'religion' and 'sin' into clearly-defined entities.[4] In an exhaustive exegesis of what he calls '[t]he religious/biblical fundamentalist anti-homosexual imperative' in contemporary Jamaica, Cecil Gutzmore cites dancehall deejays (including Beenie Man) who condemn 'homosexual behaviour as wrong in the sight of "di Almighty"' (126). Clearly, sexual identity and/or desire are matters of great moral urgency for dancehall deejays, even though this kind of religious righteousness might seem rather anomalous, and the priest/deejay coupling somewhat at odds, given the notorious – and not particularly Christian – 'slackness' of many dancehall lyrics (it is of course, possible that religious righteousness is being used as a foil for slackness and a justification for prejudice). The contradictions multiply when those who deploy Christian rhetoric to defend the vilification of queerness in Jamaica also complain of neo-colonialist intervention by international human rights and LGBTQ organisations, overlooking the fact that Christianity came to the island along with colonialism and slavery. Indeed, the notorious clause in the Jamaican constitution that proscribes 'buggery' is itself a colonial hand-me-down dating back to the nineteenth century.[5] The argument that anti-homosexuality is a local, African-Jamaican cultural phenomenon, comprehensible only to locals, sits uneasily with the Christian ideological imperative that, according to Gutzmore, constitutes one of the driving forces behind homophobic discourse in Jamaica.

Peter Tatchell was no doubt mistaken to fall back on the easy and emotive rhetorical comparison between one collective hate crime and another. The 'gassing of Jewish people' in Europe and the expression and commission of verbal and physical hate crimes against queers in Jamaica possess their own historical, political and social specificities, and it is usually unhelpful or even falsifying to elide such contexts. Homophobia is not synonymous with, or even necessarily similar to, racism; as d'bi young shows in one of her contributions to this special issue, it is an unfortunate truth that anti-racist activism does not always entail taking a stand against homophobia and/or heterocentrism. And yet, it is also true that queerness, colonialism, nationalism and heterosexuality have always and inevitably been imbricated and implicated. In *Colonial Desire*, Robert Young elucidates some of the ways in which hybridity and homosexuality were identified as perversions and forms of degeneration in colonial discourse, even though 'on the face of it . . . [biological] hybridity must always be a resolutely heterosexual category' (26). Moreover, as Young and others such as Joseph Bristow point out, 'playing the imperial game was . . . already an implicitly homo-erotic practice', since colonial anxieties surrounding racial amalgamation and degeneration seemed to encourage same-sex sex (Young 26). The correlation of same-sex desire and/or sex with perversion and perverse neo-colonial transnationalism is certainly conveyed in the *Jamaica Star* blogger's call to 'all true Jamaicans' all over the world to stand up and support Jamaican values, which presumably include 'knowing the difference' between race, religion and perversion/'sin'. As Gayatri Gopinath notes, queer desires and subjectivities are dense sites of meaning in the (re)production of notions of 'culture', 'tradition' and belonging, and they reveal the conflation of 'perverse' sexualities and diasporic affiliations within nationalist imaginaries (2). Thinking from a specifically queer diasporic epistemological and critical standpoint might usefully expose and trouble the ways in which theorisations of postcolonial diaspora identities consolidate nationalism's sexed and gendered ideologies. Positing postcolonial and diaspora identity as the queer 'other' of the nation facilitates the simultaneous critique of heterocentricity and nationalism; at the same time, it is crucial to recognise that postcolonial and diaspora discourse may well be highly invested in precisely those norms of masculinity, reproduction and genealogical descent that constitute the focus of a queer critique (Gopinath 10, 11, 32).

The critics and theorists I cited earlier have paid close attention to such 'transexions' of race, gender and nation, insisting that it is impossible to understand these discursive fields in isolation from each other, and suggesting that a queer postcolonial critique could provide a means to traverse and transform conceptual boundaries while challenging various kinds of 'identic fixity' (Harper et al 1). 'Sexuality is on the move', affirm Patton and Sánchez-Eppler in their introduction to *Queer Diasporas*, and they draw out those lines of enquiry in which universalising ideas about sexuality are deconstructed so that 'the lilt of each local articulation of desire' may be captured (2). Any discussion of what these editors call the discursive factors that come into play in the complex lamination of the local onto the global must also take care not to flatten the specificities of class and economics in the course of accounting for the forms that are assumed by desire and sexual alterity within transnational, translocal contexts (Patton, Sánchez-Eppler 2–3; Hawley 6). Again, Gopinath is correct to insist that we develop frames of analysis which are supple enough to account for transnational movements and the discourses of class, gender and sexuality with which they are coterminous (158).

Such discursive 'suppleness' may move us towards a more nuanced understanding of confrontations such as the ones that occurred in 2004 and beyond, in which the ideologies and interests of LGBTQ and postcolonial communities were (and remain) apparently irreconcilable. Taking up a queer postcolonial and/or diasporic hermeneutic standpoint might, for example, better equip us to critique the universalising assumptions that may well be at work in human rights discourse, while also alerting us to the unfortunate colonial resonances of powerful nations such as the UK and the USA withholding their capital from performers in less well-off postcolonial countries (the net losses to the music industry that were cited by OutRage!; see Oumano, Petridis). At the same time, such a critique would avoid the kind of simplistic extenuations in which it is claimed (for example) that aggressive hyper-masculinity is a colonial legacy and a symptom of present-day economic and social disempowerment in Jamaica, themselves the direct result of colonisation and imperialism. While there is certainly some truth in this kind of assertion, it does not adequately account for the vehement attitudes towards (homosexual and straight) sex expressed in some dancehall lyrics by both male and female performers, nor does it explain why these particular attitudes are expressed in this way in this place.

Male dancehall deejays have been variously hailed as priests, griots, maroons and teachers; repeated allusions to their sexual prowess and penis size suggest that these may be 'near obsessions' of theirs, along with homosexuality, bisexuality, transvestism, transsexuality, paedophilia, rape, oral sex and other 'daily' activities relating to women's bodies (Gutzmore 119).[6] Moving with apparent ease among a range of registers – pedagogical, sexual, religious, economic – these deejays seem to inhabit multiple, unstable, some might say performative as well as theatrical identities. In other words, they *themselves* appear to be ontologically elastic, border-crossing, camp, 'queer', notwithstanding the paranoid and panicked heterosexuality that they express in their lyrics.[7] Exploring dancehall as a queer postcolonial arena in which hyperbolic masculinist heterosexuality and aggressive nationality are *re*-hyperbolised in dialectical response to complaints from 'western' organisations and queers in Jamaica (whose 'Jamaican-ness' is deemed to be corrupted and degraded by virtue of their sexed and gendered identities) may not give rise to the kind of calm dialogue envisaged by Gutzmore, in which queers and homophobes '[treat] each other's positions with a certain seriousness and mutual respect' (122). Nor will this kind of analysis diminish the very real physical and verbal violence routinely faced on multiple fronts by sexual minorities in Jamaica and elsewhere.[8] A queer postcolonial reading cannot prevent border panic from occurring in the west, nor can it regulate the expression and enactment of homosexual panic in postcolonial nations; on the other hand, it may suggest interpretive possibilities in which the complexities of national, sexual, gendered and economic positionalities are acknowledged and critiqued, short-circuiting any recourse to the clichés of nationalism while also accepting the potentially problematic universalism and globalism of human rights discourse.[9] Such a hermeneutics will have no interest in staking a claim to a nationalist and/or humanist ontological ground. 'Knowing [and asserting] the difference' between 'race', sexuality ('f*g**tism' in this context), nation, religion and social class may begin to seem less pressing when it is understood that 'queer postcolonial', 'queer diaspora' and/or 'queer Jamaican' are not oxymoronic, or even dualistic, subject positions.

Exemplifying this kind of constructive instability, the writers represented in this special issue deploy many different registers and voices, occupying a number of vantage points from which to train their gaze on various geographical, historical and textual locales. So while Suniti Namjoshi playfully ventriloquises an elderly Sycorax and a queer Ariel in her narrative verse, Saradha Soobrayen's lyrical 'My Conqueror' personifies a colonised island which is ambivalently attached to its female coloniser nation. Chris Dunton's queer re-reading of a canonical postcolonial play by Wole Soyinka opens up a range of new interpretive possibilities, while Keguro Macharia has produced a remarkable blend of poetic, academic and autobiographical prose in a piece that seems self-consciously to defy generic description. Meanwhile, Jarrod Hayes gives a lucid reading of queerness, diaspora, nationalism and Zionism in his 'reviving' of Albert Memmi's penis, and he argues convincingly for the queer potential of the very concept of diaspora. None of the writers represented here express frustration that, in this context at least, they are working within a queer postcolonial textual 'bracket' (although Valerie Mason-John and Dorothea Smartt explore some of the consequences of accepting politically-loaded sobriquets such as 'lesbian' and 'black'). In contrast, while commissioning for the issue, I was surprised to find that a number of the authors I approached were wary of the 'queer' in 'queer postcolonial', regarding it as a pigeonhole that delimited and confined their writerly and personal identities in the public eye. A well-known statement by James Baldwin might provide a useful alternative to this kind of suspicion: in answer to a question about how he coped with being poor, black and gay at the beginning of his writing career, Baldwin claimed that he thought he had hit the jackpot. I am not suggesting that queer postcolonial and/or queer diaspora necessarily constitute a 'jackpot' in the same way that 'poor, black and gay' apparently did for Baldwin. Nonetheless, in different modes and from myriad perspectives, the pieces collected in this special issue constitute an affirmation or even a celebration of queer postcolonial subject positions and hermeneutics, as well as a challenge to the kind of reductive stereotypical thinking that would treat class, race, gender and sexuality as discrete, separable entities. Perhaps we may be permitted to revise Homi Bhabha's echo of Toni Morrison via Salman Rushdie by asserting that the truest eye now belongs to the *queer* migrant's doubled, tripled, infinitely multiplied, vision (Bhabha 5).

Sara Salih

## Notes

1   For newspaper reports about the events of 2004, see *Guardian*, 16 Aug. 2004, 25 Aug. 2004, 3 Nov. 2004, 10 Dec. 2004; *Jamaica Gleaner*, 27 June 2004, *Jamaica Observer*, 16 July 2004, *New York Times*, 6 Sept. 2004, *Village Voice*, 15 Feb. 2005.

2   Ann Laura Stoler's work has also been influential in this field (see especially *Race and the Education of Desire*). See also Diana Fuss's important analysis of Fanon's disquieting discussions of femininity and homosexuality. Fuss, 154.

3   Many of these arguments are rehearsed in Cooper (although she is not responding directly to the events under discussion here); see Cooper (especially, 39, 153, 160, 168, 178) for discussions concerning 'insider' readings of 'indigenous cultural texts like Buju Banton's "Boom By By"' (168). Cooper argues that such texts have been 'taken all too literally out of context' by non-native 'outsiders who do not understand the multi-track discourse of the dancehall' (39). According to Cooper, an increasingly empowered 'outernational massive – the gay community' (47) and 'powerful organizations of homosexuals in the North Atlantic like GLAAD seem to be playing the role of imperial overlords in the cultural arena', so that Jamaican deejays must often 'run for cover' (177). On the other hand, '"[h]omophobia" in neo-African societies like Jamaica is often conceived as an articulation of an Africanist worldview . . . [and] an affirmation of Afrocentric norms of sexual propriety' (163). Cooper concludes that 'the battle for the fundamental transformation of Jamaican society must first be fought and won on native soil' (178), and that although '[m]ost male homosexuals in Jamaica seem content to remain in the proverbial closet . . . the door is wide open' (162). Notwithstanding the claim made by Cooper and others that 'lyrical violence' and actual violence have no connection to one another, in 2005 Buju Banton was charged with – and acquitted of – participating in an attack against six gay men in Jamaica; and his virulent but enduringly popular 'Boom Bye Bye' was allegedly sung at the murder scene of Brian Williams, Jamaica's leading gay activist, in 2004. See Sanneh and Ireland.

4   The choice of suffix in that curious, and curiously self-censored, nonce noun 'faggotism', suggests a quality (eg chauvinism), or a belief system (eg Puritanism), or a doctrinal stance (eg fanaticism), rather than a sexed/gendered identity, or even a group of sexual acts that would putatively define this 'faggotism'. Why not 'faggotry', as in the 'buggery' that is proscribed in the Jamaican constitution; or, one is tempted to say, as in the 'bigotry' of such attitudes?

5   'Jamaica (Constitution) Order in Council, 1962', chapter 3, section 76, specifies that 'the abominable crime of buggery' is punishable by imprisonment and ten years maximum hard labour. Section 43 groups 'buggery, either with mankind or with any animal' under 'menaces', along with rape and assault. In *Laws of Jamaica* vol. XXIX.

6    See *Guardian*, 6 Aug. 2004, for a review of Beenie Man's *Back To Basics*. According to the reviewer, now that Beenie Man has given up violence against queers as a 'lyrical topic', he is left only with the subject of his penis.

7    Although she does not read dancehall as a queer space, Donna Hope identifies an increasing emphasis on male external appearance in dancehall culture. As a result, 'the borders between masculine and feminine aesthetics, costuming and public display have become blurred, and men in the dancehall have striven to display their personhood'. Hope sees 'global factors' contributing to the subtle recreation of gendered norms in Jamaican dancehall culture, to the extent that men now practise formerly tabooed 'feminine' aesthetics and rituals, such as visiting cosmetologists for facials, manicures and pedicures. Hope's observations suggest the aptness of a reading of dancehall as queer ('The British Link-Up Crew', 108–09).

8    In this context, it is worth noting that the Human Rights Watch report, 'Hated to Death: Homophobia, Violence, and Jamaica's HIV/AIDS Epidemic' cited religious intolerance, Jamaican popular music and the use of anti-gay slogans and rhetoric by political leaders as causal factors of the violence against queers in Jamaica (12–13).

9    cf. Michael Warner's observation in his introduction to *fear of Queer Planet*, that as gay activists from non-western contexts become more and more involved in setting political agendas, and as the rights discourse of internationalism is extended to more and more cultural contexts, Anglo American queer theorists will have to be more alert to the globalising – and localising – tendencies of our theoretical languages (xii).

## Works Cited

ARIEL. *A Review of International English Literature* 30.2 (1999).

Bhabha, Homi. *The Location of Culture*. London: Routledge, 1994.

Branigan, Tania. 'Reggae Star Beenie Man Could Face Charges for "Homophobic" Lyrics'. *Guardian* 16 Aug. 2004.

Clunis, Andrew. 'London Pressures Dancehall Stars'. *Jamaica Gleaner* 27 June 2004.

Cooper, Carolyn. *Soundclash. Jamaican Culture at Large*. Basingstoke: Palgrave Macmillan, 2004.

Dollimore, Jonathan. *Sexual Dissidence. Augustine to Wilde, Freud to Foucault*. Oxford: Oxford UP, 1991.

Fuss, Diana. *Identification Papers*. London: Routledge, 1995.

Gopinath, Gayatri. *Impossible Desires. Queer Diasporas and South Asian Public Cultures*. Durham: Duke UP, 2005.

Gutzmore, Cecil. 'Casting the First Stone! Policing of Homo/sexuality in Jamaican Popular Culture'. *Interventions* 6.1 (2004): 118–34.

Harper, Phillip Brian, Anne McClintock, José Estaban Muñoz, and Trish Rosen. 'Queer Transexions of Race, Nation and Gender'. Spec. issue of *Social Text* 52–53.3–4 (1997).

Hawley, John C., ed. *Post-Colonial, Queer. Theoretical Intersections*. New York: SUNY Press, 2001.

Hope, Donna P. 'Clash – Gays vs Dancehall'. *Jamaica Gleaner* 5 Oct. 2004.

——. 'The British Link-Up Crew. Consumption Masquerading as Masculinity in the Dancehall'. *Interventions* 6.1 (2004): 101–17.

Human Rights Watch. 'Hated to Death. Homophobia, Violence, and Jamaica's HIV/AIDS Epidemic'. 16. 6 (B), Nov. 2004.

Ireland, Doug. 'Jamaica, Island of Hate'. *Gay City*, 5.40, 5–11 Oct. 2006.

Johnson, E. Patrick, and Mae G. Henderson, eds. *Black Queer Studies. A Critical Anthology*. Durham: Duke UP, 2005.

Laville, Sandra. 'Barman's Murder Brings Call to Ban Homophobic Singer'. *Guardian* 3 Nov. 2004.

Muñoz, José Estaban. *Disidentifications. Queers of Color and the Performance of Politics*. Minnesota: Minnesota UP, 1999.

Oumano, Elena. 'Jah Division'. *Village Voice* 15 Feb. 2005.

Patton, Cindy and Benigno Sánchez-Eppler. *Queer Diasporas*. Durham: Duke UP, 2000.

Petridis, Alexis. 'Pride and Prejudice'. *Guardian* 10 Dec. 2004.

'Reggae Activist Needed'. *Jamaica Star* 11 Oct. 2004.

Sanneh, Kelefa. 'Dancehall's Vicious Side: Anti-gay Attitudes'. *New York Times* 6 Sept. 2004.

Somerville, Siobhan B. *Queering the Colour Line. Race and the Invention of Homosexuality in American Culture*. Durham: Duke UP, 2000.

Stoler, Ann Laura. *Race and the Education of Desire. Foucault's* History of Sexuality *and the Colonial Order of Things*. Durham: Duke UP, 1995.

Walters, Basil. 'Are Dancehall Artistes Going to Bow?' *Jamaica Observer* 16 July 2004.

Warner, Michael, ed. *Fear of a Queer Planet. Queer Politics and Social Theory*. Minneapolis: Minnesota UP, 1993.

Wilson, Jamie. 'Gay Groups Call for Rejection of Stars "Who Back Murder"'. *Guardian* 25 Aug. 2004.

Young, Robert J. C. *Colonial Desire. Hybridity in Theory, Culture and Race*. London: Routledge, 1995.

# Circumcising Zionism, Queering Diaspora

## REVIVING ALBERT MEMMI'S PENIS

**Jarrod Hayes**

'The Diaspora must cease to be a Diaspora.' With these words, the Jewish Tunisian writer Albert Memmi places his hope for Jewish liberation in the realisation of the Zionist project through the modern state of Israel (*Liberation* 286). Memmi would later confirm his assertion of the Israeli state as the essence of Jewishness: 'Israel is the heart and the head. Israel is now our heart of hearts ... but the Diaspora is the great, suffering body' (*Jews* 67). Through a mind/body binary, Memmi presents diasporic identities as degraded, inauthentic, as the corporeal supplement to a Jewish essence. This understanding of Jewishness stands in stark contrast with anti-Semitic racialisations of Jews as pure embodiment (see Gilman), but is Memmi's project the only possible route towards Jewish liberation? For those for whom diaspora *is* the 'essence' of Jewish identity, would Memmi's project not signify annihilation? Memmi himself states that 'the existence of a Jewish nation will at last permit the disappearance of Jewishness' (*Liberation* 301). According to Ammiel Alcalay, state Zionism is founded on precisely such a desire: 'Official discourse spoke matter-of-factly of the "elimination of the Diaspora", a slogan that even slipped into the "elimination of the Jews"' (221).[1] When Memmi writes, '[T]he Jew has to find a *total solution*' (*Liberation* 277), he not only suggests the disturbing implications of the 'disappearance' he envisions, but also conjures up a resonance with the final solution.

Yet, whereas Memmi understands returning to Israel as a remedy for the uprootedness that characterises his vision of diaspora, in this essay I seek out alternative returns within Memmi's work itself. Memmi did not come to his explicitly pro-Zionist position right away. He was first known for his theorisation of the situation of the colonised, his anti-colonial writings and his support for *Arab* nationalism. His first essays, included in *Portrait du colonisé, précédé de Portrait du colonisateur* (1957, *The Colonizer and the Colonized*), are

directly related to his first, semi-autobiographical novel — *La Statue de sel* (1953, *The Pillar of Salt*). In this *Bildungsroman*, Memmi revives Jewish identity through a different kind of narrative, which plants roots not in Palestine, but in a predominantly Arab North Africa. In a later interview, Memmi would redeploy the same heart/mind rhetoric used to describe Israel above: '[M]any of my readers ... themselves have a Hara in their hearts and minds' (*Terre* 12, my trans.). Here, however, he reverses his previous associations, so that the Hara − Tunis's Jewish quarter − becomes the heart and reason of Jewish identity. This statement conjures up the ghosts that haunt Memmi's Zionism, ghosts of the very diaspora he has condemned to death.

Whereas Memmi's return to a collective past in the Hara might at first seem to parallel Zionist narratives that claim to return the Nation of Israel to its pre-diaspora origins, by reading Memmi's first novel against his later Zionist essays, one can revive the ghosts of a diasporic body left to die in the latter.[2] And this body returns with its Jewishness inscribed onto the site of the circumcised penis, a site of difference from and connection with the Arab world of which Memmi is a part. If Alcalay describes a body of Arab Jewish texts from Israel in which the promised land has become a land of uprootedness and broken promises, Memmi's early fiction re-roots Jewish identity in a Hara of the mind. If Alcalay 'remakes Levantine culture' (to quote his subtitle) by deconstructing the Arab/Jew opposition, Memmi situates this Levant in a reconceived Mediterranean culture in which Orient/West and North/South binaries are also undone. Traditionally, the circumcised penis is a sign of man's alliance with God; it is thus the place where a phallocentric genealogy is inscribed onto the male body, making him a member of the Nation of Israel. (As Howard Eilberg-Schwartz writes, 'one must have a member to be a member' [145]). Yet this site upon which patriarchy is founded nonetheless signifies the potential for its undoing, for circumcision also marks the feminisation of the male Israelite

*Wasafiri Vol. 22, No. 1 March 2007, pp. 6–11*
ISSN 0269-0055 print/ISSN 1747-1508 online © 2007 Wasafiri
http://www.tandf.co.uk/journals    DOI: 10.1080/02690050601097542

and therefore the threat of negating the masculinity that undergirds the Zionism upon which the Israeli state is founded. By bringing the emasculated diasporic penis back to life, therefore – that is, by bringing it back from the past as well as reviving it as a source of pleasure – *The Pillar of Salt* reroutes Jewish identity through alternative roots, which will also serve here as my point of departure for some reflections on the emerging field of queer diaspora studies.[3]

Memmi's work can thus be situated in relation to a body of writing on Jewish masculinity. In *The Jew's Body,* for example, Sander Gilman examines anti-Semitic constructions of the Jewish male body as feminised and therefore degenerate. Conversely, both Daniel Boyarin (in '"This We Know to Be the Carnal Israel": Circumcision and the Erotic Life of God and Israel') and Eilberg-Schwartz (in *God's Phallus and Other Problems for Men and Monotheism*) seek to reclaim this femininity in an explicitly feminist reconceptualisation of Jewish masculinity by valorising what anti-Semitic discourses abject, and recuperating the traditional feminisation of men in biblical and rabbinic writings. Both have also described circumcision as a key component of this feminisation. Boyarin describes circumcision as making the Jewish man 'open to receive the divine speech and vision of God' (495). Since 'God is the husband to Israel the wife' (97), according to Eilberg-Schwartz, 'men may meet God only as women. And circumcision makes them desirable women' (174). Boyarin discusses more recent implications of this feminisation in *Unheroic Conduct: The Rise of Heterosexuality and the Invention of the Jewish Man.* Although he is careful to limit his findings to Ashkenazi traditions and warns against seeing a continuity in the parallel between ancient and rabbinic writings on the one hand and pre-nineteenth-century northern European Jewish cultures on the other, his conclusions are nonetheless relevant for understanding Memmi's relation to Zionism. For the consolidation of Zionism in nineteenth-century Europe required a repudiation of this feminisation to assert Israel as a nation of manly men among nations of men. Given that the Zionist state establishes an Ashkenazi hegemony at the expense of Arab Jews, the parallel feminised diasporic body in Memmi's early fiction, without explicitly resisting the Zionist masculinisation that finds its epitome in Max Nordau's 'Muscle-Jew', nonetheless returns to haunt this masculinisation.[4]

*The Pillar of Salt*'s narrative is framed as the childhood memories of its narrator Alexandre Mordekhaï Benillouche. The chapter 'At the *Kouttab* School' offers a *mise-en-abîme* of this retrospective structure when Alexandre, after witnessing a peculiar scene in a streetcar as a high-school student, looks back on an earlier childhood episode within the overall looking back of the novel. In the streetcar episode, a grocer from the island of Djerba singles out a two-year-old Muslim boy for teasing after inquiring whether he is circumcised. When the boy's father says no, the grocer attempts to 'purchase' the boy's penis at higher and higher prices and, after a series of more and more adamant refusals, reaches into the boy's pants and pretends to snatch his penis without

paying. In this lesson of phallic privilege, the little boy fights off the aggressor and defends his penis against the threat of castration.

Even as the game begins, the narrator identifies with its victim across ethno-confessional lines:

> Quite obviously, the boy knew this whole routine and had already heard the same proposition before. I too, knew it all, and had myself played the game some years ago, attacked by other aggressors and feeling the same emotions of shame [and sexual excitement, of revolt and complicitous curiosity]. The child's eyes sparkled with the pleasure of his awareness of his own growing virility, and with the shock of his revolt against such an unwarranted attack. (167; 186)[5]

This identification is so strong that the narrator experiences a physical sensation in his penis, which he takes to be the same as what the little boy is feeling:

> When the boy in the streetcar screamed with fear, I felt my own [sex] quiver as if in response to a [call surging] suddenly from the depths of my own childhood . . . Yes, I know well that unpleasant but voluptuous [shiver]. Before going to grade school, I used to go to the *kouttab* . . . . (169–70; 188)

This sensation, like that evoked by the Proustian Madeleine, revives an identical feeling from his much earlier past, thereby bringing an entire scene into the present. One day at the *kouttab*, or Hebrew school, after the rabbi leaves the room, a class of boys decides to stage a circumcision ceremony. They choose the smallest among them to be circumcised, and yet again, Memmi's narrator identifies with the frightened victim, so totally in fact that he experiences the very same fear:

> But the mere threat had bound me closely to the victim and [set off inside me] all the terrors of a real calvary. I could feel the anguish of the small boy who, all trembling, was now being carried, like the sacrificial lamb, on the shoulders of our [monitor]. (172–73; 191)

Since the boy is already circumcised, the excitement that drives their play-acting is, to a great extent, the tension and fear that the boy might 'really' be 'circumcised' again, which would necessarily involve the removal of something other than a foreskin:

> My heart beat faster, under the pressure of fear and [embarrassed] emotion. . . . Were they really going to cut off his penis? The mere though of it gave me a vague but not unpleasant pain in my [groin]. (173; 192)

He again experiences this identification as a physical sensation at the site of his own penis, which tingles with excitement. This scene ends climactically, and quite literally so, since the narrator describes his own reaction as an explosion of *jouissance:*

> It was physically intolerable, and I felt truly faint when the High Priest's right hand, armed with a razor, came slowly down toward the tiny bit of white flesh that [protruded] between the index and the second finger of his left hand.
>   But my sense of having been liberated was sudden, and all my fear vanished explosively, together with my shame, my [jouissance], my disgust, and the unbearable tension that was born of the anguished silence of all of us: unable to stand it any longer, the victim had just burst into tears. (174–75; 193)

These passages could serve as textbook examples of what D Boyarin has called 'Jewissance', a pleasure that comes from 'an extraordinary richness of experience and a powerful sense of being rooted somewhere in the world, in a world of memory, intimacy, and connectedness' (*Unheroic* xxiii). Jewissance *à la* Memmi is much more concrete than Boyarin's pleasures of the mind and of being a member of a collective identity; Memmi's Jewissance is a physical pleasure emanating *from* his member:

> [In my sex, I felt this voluptuous fear translate into electric shivers.] How shall I ever forget my complicity? Yes, I was playing my part in the ceremony, in the ancestral and collective ritual that was food for the mind. (174; 193)

In fact, Memmi's Jewissance is a *jouissance* in *all* the meanings of the word; *il jouit de sa judéité.* That is, he enjoys, benefits from, and relishes in his Jewishness, which also makes him cum. In this passage, at least, the liberation of a particular Jew ('my sense of being liberated') takes on quite different contours from those outlined in *The Liberation of the Jew.* Furthermore, his penis not only makes him quintessentially Jewish, but also connects him to other penises, those of other Jewish men. Though his circumcised penis inserts him into a phallic understanding of Jewish identity, however, the circumcision that writes this Jewishness onto his penis also signifies his emasculation: '[M]y groin ached [at the same spot,] as if the knife were about to wound me' (*Pillar* 174; 193). And although the narrator shares this threat, the possibility of castration is an inextricable component of his physical pleasure.

Yet whereas his circumcised penis is supposedly what defines him as Jewish (and being Jewish supposedly means he cannot be Christian or Muslim), it actually gives him an *intimate* connection with those from whom he is supposed to be different. The most intimate connection is reserved for the Muslim penis, which tingles in complete sync with the narrator's own (at least as the two are brought together in the imaginary space created through remembrance). For identification with/through the penis is a tactile process: 'Will I ever be able to forget the Orient, since it is grafted into my

flesh, and it is enough to touch myself to verify its definitive mark?' (188 in the French, my trans.). And we remember that it is indeed by touching the uncircumcised penis that the Djerbian (and through him, the other men present) participates in a collective experience of circumcision. In the space of the streetcar, '[a]ll the races of our city were represented' (166): 'Decidedly, among Mediterraneans, we felt like family' (187 in the French, my trans.). This rhetoric of kinship unites Jewish, Muslim, French, Bedouin, Sicilian and Djerbian, and it is precisely this genealogy, this 'Orient ... grafted into my flesh', that marks his penis not only with Jewish difference, but also as being in relation with non-Jewish Mediterraneans. The streetcar thus serves as a metaphor for a diasporic Jewish identity, for in it Alexandre experiences his Jewissance as he and his fellow travellers (get in) touch (with) their penises along the shared routes to their identities rooted in collective memories. The streetcar scene might therefore be read as a circle jerk in which Memmi's narrator only gets in touch with his Jewishness by figuratively touching other penises.

In a later chapter of *The Pillar of Salt*, this figurative contact is literalised in Memmi's characterisation of the homoerotic nature of a specifically Mediterranean sexuality:

> I had never been able to [approve of] the sexual games of boys. When I was told that one of the older pupils offered to caress, with enough skill to cause an orgasm [jusqu'à la jouissance], anyone who wished, I refused with scorn and horror. My comrades organized these parties of collective pleasure out on a vacant lot not far from the school. Apparently, they all lined up with their back[s] to the wall and Giacomo passed [in front of them] one by one. I was the only one in the [lounge for the boarders' monitors] not to talk of my adventures or to describe with [self-indulgence] the sexual attributes of men and women a thousand times a day. To me, such promiscuity was [in very bad taste]; besides, what had I to tell? (239–40; 257–58)

As in the streetcar scene, here both Northern and Southern Mediterraneans share a sexuality that is most notable for its lack of a clear distinction between homo- and heterosexuality. Yet, the very passage that admits the homoerotic nature of this community of men bound through the connections they feel in their penises serves to deny the narrator's participation in its homoeroticism. Furthermore, Alexandre certainly knows a lot about something he has supposedly never done, enough to repeat in great detail descriptions from which he apparently recoiled in horror.

In a previous reading of these and other passages from *The Pillar of Salt*, I situated these erotic scenarios from Alexandre's past within the novel's narrative of colonial assimilation and alienation (*Queer Nations* 243–47, 253–55, 277–86). There, I understood Memmi's denial of being implicated in the 'parties of collective pleasure' as part of a narrative of sexual development that parallels the civilising process of Alexandre's colonial assimilation. As Memmi's narrator leaves behind the dark continent of a primitive past, of a childhood marked as polymorphously perverse, he comes closer to achieving the goal of French education for the colonised. Yet *The Pillar of Salt* quite clearly details the price of such an assimilation — alienation. At the end of this novel, framed as the memories recalled during an exam, Alexandre turns away from French civilisation altogether when he decides not to hand in the exam he has been taking, thereby calling into question his previous choice of Western over Tunisian culture: 'I had refused the Orient and the West was refusing me' (352–53 in the French, my trans.). This reversal, this rejection of his previous rejection of the 'Orient' (itself a colonial construct) thus logically implies overturning his rejection of 'Oriental sex' in the above passage. The very narrative structure of the novel, therefore, brings the remembered childhood into conflict with its framing (the French educational system and its civilising mission), brings the queerness of the past into conflict with the present. In other words, the novel not only represents queer childhood episodes, but also offers a narrative structure for queering the present by returning *to* the past and returning the past to the present.

In that earlier reading, I stressed the implications of this queer haunting for *Tunisian* nationalism, since the Jewish presence revived in *The Pillar of Salt* comes to contest a politics of purity that would define the Maghrebian nation as Arab and Muslim. My point in this essay has been to carry out a parallel reading of Memmi in relation to Zionism, in relation to Israeli as opposed to Tunisian nationalism. For inasmuch as the Zionism that led to the Israeli state claims to return the Nation of Israel to the promised land, it is not merely a revival of the past or a return to roots; it is also a narrative of progress, of gendered progress, one that requires the masculinisation of its men in relation to (other) European nations. No matter how many Zionist essays Memmi pens, the emasculated 'Oriental' penis of his first novel will always stand in contrast with the gendered politics of Zionism described by Daniel Boyarin and resisted by both Daniel and Jonathan Boyarin in their more explicitly anti-Zionist writings. This rather queer penis may also provide one way of understanding the potentially queer role of diaspora within what James Clifford calls 'a *diasporist* anti-Zionism' of which, for him, the Boyarins and Alcalay serve as prime examples (326).

In their jointly authored 'Diaspora: Generation and the Ground of Jewish Identity', D and J Boyarin propose an alternative 'genealogy' of Jewish identity, one based on diaspora as a counter to Zionism.[6] In direct opposition with the passages from Memmi's essays with which I began and with what Ella Shohat calls 'the Zionist rejection of the Diaspora' (272), they retrieve a biblically-based model of Jewish identity in which diaspora and connection with a homeland are not at odds. For 'the biblical story is not one of autochthony but one of always already coming from somewhere else' ('Diaspora' 715). In other words, dispersal in biblical narratives always *precedes* the promised land, not the

reverse; one does not return to a promised land from which one has been expelled as one would return to a rooted essence. In their introduction to *Queer Diasporas*, Cindy Patton and Benigno Sánchez-Eppler root their account of queer diaspora in an even prior dispersal, that of Adam and Eve from Eden (2). Although they read Genesis as a foundation myth for heterosexuality, they simultaneously queer it by understanding the appearance of Eve as disrupting a homosocial bond between Adam and God. While the editors then move on quickly to questions of migration – particularly the migrations from country to city so crucial to the development of community and identity in the dominant narratives of lesbian and gay studies – this foundational moment in queer diaspora studies has an unexplored potential. Perhaps unknowingly, Patton and Sánchez-Eppler thus conflate pre-lapsarian paradise with the promised land as the site of pre-diasporic origins, but this confusion might nonetheless serve as a productive reminder of what the Boyarins refer to as 'always already coming from somewhere else'. Read through Memmi, and the work of the Boyarins and others, Patton and Sánchez-Eppler's queering of Genesis reminds us that there is no 'before the dispersal' except in a mythical origin that is always already marked as unobtainable, unreconstitutable.

*Queer Diasporas* is one of first published texts in the field of queer diaspora studies. (Others include Manalansan; Cruz-Malavé and Manalansan; and La Fountain-Stokes.) In *Impossible Desires: Queer Diasporas and South Asian Public Cultures*, Gayatri Gopinath offers what is perhaps the most explicit definition of 'queer disapora'. According to her, within the nationalist discourses of the South Asian diasporic elite, 'queerness is to heterosexuality as the diaspora is to the nation':

> If within heteronormative logic the queer is seen as the debased and inadequate copy of the heterosexual, so too is diaspora within nationalist logic positioned as the queer Other of the nation, its inauthentic imitation. (11)

For Gopinath, therefore, 'queer diaspora' is the critical practice that serves 'to trouble and denaturalize the close relationship between nationalism and heterosexuality' (11). To draw attention to the need for queering diaspora, Gopinath points to the gendered and sexual implications of the term *diaspora* itself. Stefan Helmreich explains that the term *diaspora* 'comes from the Greek διασπορα (dispersion), from δια (through) + σπειρειν (to sow or scatter)' (245).[7] Even in its most restrictive sense – to describe Jewish, Greek and Armenian diasporas – the term carries sexual implications in that it 'summons up the image of scattered seeds', which 'are metaphorical for the male "substance" that is traced in genealogical histories' (245). Furthermore,

> [t]he word 'sperm' is etymologically connected to diaspora [, which] in its traditional sense, thus refers

us to a system of kinship reckoned through men and suggests the questions of legitimacy in paternity that patriarchy generates. (245)

Clifford's assertion that '[d]iasporic experiences are always gendered' (313) is thus quite an understatement. The very concept of diaspora itself implies a masculinist definition of the relation between community and origins. The patrilineality implied by the term and upon which the notion of diaspora frequently relies nonetheless frequently remains hidden whenever the term is evoked.

In Gopinath's specific context, again, nation and diaspora are seen as much more compatible (at least in the hegemonic models of diasporism she critiques) than within Zionist discourses. Her retrieval of queerness within diaspora thus leads directly to a queering of the nation. It is probably the case, however, that diaspora haunts the nation differently for Zionism, which actually envisions the elimination of diaspora. One can thus not only locate queerness within the diaspora, but also understand diaspora as having a queer relation to Israel (as both biblical nation and modern state). In contrast with Gopinath's project, Memmi's retrieval of the Jewish diaspora as queer helps to imagine the undoing of Zionism as a political project (as opposed to queering the Israeli state) by allowing the rhizomatic connections of diaspora to return in the process of returning to origins in a homeland of the mind (as opposed to a physical territory already inhabited by Palestinians). Memmi thus allows us to carry forward Gopinath's queering of diaspora by helping us to tease out the queer potential of the very concept of diaspora itself.

While Memmi's revival of his penis relies on the same phallic genealogy Helmreich alludes to, his Jewissance entails spilling his seed rather differently. Indeed, it is not through heterosexual reproduction that he plants the seeds for a Zionist state; rather, the promised land flows forth like milk and honey every time he touches himself 'to verify [the] definitive mark [of the Orient]'. J and D Boyarin retrieve a feminised diasporic anti-Zionism by performing 'the double mark of the male Jew', that is, their circumcision and head-covering, thereby undoing the body/mind opposition Memmi's Zionism relies on ('Self-Exposure' 16–22).[8] Yet whereas they *write* (about) their penises, Memmi has a wank. Indeed, 'the covenant with God was of a sexual nature' for Memmi (*Pillar* 171). But instead of getting in touch with *God* as he touches himself, Memmi touches (the penises of) fellow Arabs. The home of Jewish identity is thus not a state that pushes out the Other; rather Muslim and Jewish penises rub together in an acknowledgement that they both share an alliance with God signed by Abraham. The Nation of Israel that comes into being through a kind of circle jerk with (other) Arabs makes for a rather queer Zionism, which is more like no Zionism at all.

Indeed, Memmi shows us that the very narrative structure upon which Zionism relies offers a strategy for its undoing. The gesture of looking back is itself evoked by the novel's title; *The Pillar of Salt* is a biblical reference to Lot's wife who – disobeying God's command not to look back on a burning

Sodom – turns into a pillar of salt. Memmi explicitly connects his fate to hers:

> I am dying [from] having turned back [on my]self. It is forbidden to see oneself, and I have [finished knowing] myself. [Like Lot's wife, whom God turned into a pillar of salt, can I still live beyond my gaze]? (335; 368)

Since Memmi looks back on himself as Lot's wife looked upon Sodom, he equates his own past with Sodom. Furthermore, Memmi's use of the verb *to know* recalls the very reason for Sodom's destruction:

> [T]he men of Sodom, compassed the house round ... And they called unto Lot, and said unto him, Where are the men which came in to thee this night? bring them out unto us, that we may know them. (Gen. 19: 4–5)

Memmi's use of 'knowing' can thus also be read in the biblical sense. When knowing oneself is the equivalent of touching oneself (which is the equivalent of touching the penises of other Jews and Arabs), the mind/body binary upon which Memmi founds his explicitly Zionist position begins to collapse as surely as the city of Sodom. As with the Hara, however, there will always be a Sodom of the mind. 'Next year in Jerusalem', then, can become the equivalent of 'Tonight in Sodom', as Zion surges from every wank in a certain streetcar of the mind, a streetcar named desire.

### Notes
1 Alcalay is quoting Segev (117–18).
2 The expression 'Nation of Israel' will be used throughout this essay in its biblical sense to distinguish it from the modern Israeli state.
3 'Dealing equally with the significance of roots and routes' is one way Paul Gilroy reconceives Africana studies through the concept of diaspora (190).
4 On Nordau, see Gilman (53–54) and D Boyarin (*Unheroic*, 76–77, 277).
5 Where I have altered (in brackets) the published translation, the second page reference is to the French original.
6 They also explicitly link their reclaiming of male femininity with this rerouting of Jewish roots (J Boyarin and D Boyarin, 'Self-Exposure'). See also J Boyarin (*Palestine*) for an example of his individual contribution to anti-Zionist writing.
7 Gopinath (5) also quotes Helmreich.
8 This essay (35) also offers a brief discussion of *The Pillar of Salt*, one J Boyarin includes in *Thinking in Jewish* (58–60).

### Works Cited
Alcalay, Ammiel. *After Jews and Arabs: Remaking Levantine Culture.* Minneapolis: U of Minnesota P, 1993.
Boyarin, Daniel. '"This We Know to Be the Carnal Israel": Circumcision and the Erotic Life of God and Israel'. *Critical Inquiry* 18.3 (1992): 474–505.

———. *Unheroic Conduct: The Rise of Heterosexuality and the Invention of the Jewish Man*. Berkeley: U of California P, 1997.

Boyarin, Daniel, and Jonathan Boyarin. 'Diaspora: Generation and the Ground of Jewish Identity'. *Critical Inquiry* 19.4 (1993): 693–725.

Boyarin, Jonathan. *Palestine and Jewish History: Criticism at the Borders of Ethnography*. Minneapolis: U of Minnesota P, 1996.

———. *Thinking in Jewish*. Chicago: U of Chicago P, 1996.

Boyarin, Jonathan, and Daniel Boyarin. 'Self-Exposure as Theory: The Double Mark of the Male Jew'. *Rhetorics of Self-Making*. Ed. Debbora Battaglia. Berkeley: U of California P, 1995. 16–42.

Clifford, James. 'Diasporas'. *Cultural Anthropology* 9.3 (1994): 302–38.

Cruz-Malavé, Arnaldo, and Martin F. Manalansan IV, eds. *Queer Globalizations: Citizenship and the Afterlife of Colonialism*. New York: New York UP, 2002.

Eilberg-Schwartz, Howard. *God's Phallus and Other Problems for Men and Monotheism*. Boston: Beacon, 1994.

Gilman, Sander. *The Jew's Body*. New York: Routledge, 1991.

Gilroy, Paul. *The Black Atlantic: Modernity and Double Consciousness*. Cambridge: Harvard UP, 1993.

Gopinath, Gayatri. *Impossible Desires: Queer Diasporas and South Asian Public Cultures*. Durham: Duke UP, 2005.

Hayes, Jarrod. *Queer Nations: Marginal Sexualities in the Maghreb*. Chicago: U of Chicago P, 2000.

Helmreich, Stefan. 'Kinship, Nation, and Paul Gilroy's Concept of Diaspora'. *Diaspora* 2.2 (1992): 243–49.

La Fountain-Stokes, Lawrence M. *Queer Ricans: Cultures and Sexualities in the Diaspora*. Minneapolis: U of Minnesota P, forthcoming.

Manalansan, Martin F., IV. *Global Divas: Filipino Gay Men in the Diaspora*. Durham: Duke UP, 2003.

Memmi, Albert. *The Colonizer and the Colonized*. Trans. Howard Greenfeld. New York: Orion, 1965.

———. *Jews and Arabs*. Trans. Eleanor Levieux. Chicago: O'Hara, 1975.

———. *Juifs et Arabes*. Paris: Gallimard, 1974.

———. *La Libération du Juif*. Paris: Gallimard, 1966.

———. *The Liberation of the Jew*. Trans. Judy Hyun. New York: Orion, 1966.

———. *The Pillar of Salt*. Trans. Edouard Roditi. New York: Criterion, 1955.

———. *Portrait du colonisé, précédé de Portrait du colonisateur*. 1957. Paris: Gallimard, 1985.

———. *La Statue de sel*. 1953. Paris: Gallimard, 1966. Coll. Folio.

———. *La Terre intérieure: Entretiens avec Victor Malka*. Paris: Gallimard, 1976.

Patton, Cindy, and Benigno Sánchez-Eppler, eds. *Queer Diasporas*. Durham: Duke UP, 2000.

Segev, Tom. *1949: The First Israelis*. New York: The Free P, 1986.

Shohat, Ella. *Israeli Cinema: East/West and the Politics of Representation*. Austin: U of Texas P, 1989.

# Saradha Soobrayen

## Like cold air passing through lips

I shall think of you as my ventriloquist,
lying under the cedar trees. Your lips
unreadable, my mouth daydreaming:
journey, draining, geranium.
My head heavy with more rhymes than sleep,
resting on your arm, near the shadow's edge.
The fragrance of wood neither green
nor brown, but shallow blue.
Your compliments lodged in me
like harvest mice nesting under leaves,
foxgloves at our feet, the north winds singing.
My ear as dumb as corn and too far gone,
to catch your heart closing like a gate behind me.

## On the water meadows

I blame the twilight for coming too soon,
not allowing enough time for you
to drown without dying. And now
the water boatmen skate on the skin
of water, we should have practised
how to breathe. Instead we undressed
each other slowly: middle names, first
loves, spiders, toads and newts. Taking our
time to visit every corner, all the while
knowing we would soon run out of self.
I want to ignore the silver scar
on your left retina: the imprint of an iceberg.
Those places you were yearning for: Bermuda,
Pacific, Icelandic waters. Confident diver

that you are, land was never your best side.
What remains is the space around
your hands, their quietness, and at the tips
of fingers the faint hum of blue.

## My Conqueror

She circles me with her Portuguese compass
and settles just long enough to quench her thirst.
She discards my Arabian name *Dina Arobi*,
and calls me *Cerné*, from island of the swans.

With the hunger of a thousand Dutch sailors
and a tongue as rough as a sea biscuit she stakes
a longer claim and makes herself comfy,
bringing her own Javanese deer, pigs and chickens.

Defending her lust for breasts and thighs, she
     blames
the ship's rats for sucking the Dodo from its shell.
Looking past my ebony limbs, she sees carved boxes
and *marron* hands at work stripping my forests.

She renames me in honour of Prince Maurice
of Nassau. A good choice, sure to scare off pirates
keen to catch a bite of river shrimp, flamed in rum.
Disheartened by cyclones and rat bites, she departs.

For eleven years, I belong to no one. I sleep
to the purring of turtledoves. Sheltered by a circle
of coral reef, my oval shape rises
from the coast up to the peaks of mountains.

A westerly wind carries her back. She unbuttons
her blue naval jacket slowly and takes me.

*Wasafiri Vol. 22, No. 1 March 2007, pp. 12–13*
ISSN 0269-0055 print/ISSN 1747-1508 online © 2007 Wasafiri
http://www.tandf.co.uk/journals      DOI: 10.1080/02690050601097559

I am her *Île de France*, her *petit pain*.
She brings spaniels. She captures *marrons*

who are pinned down and flogged, each time they run.
She takes her fill in Port Louis, shipping casks
of pure sweetness to the tea-drinking ladies of Europe.
Young Baudelaire jumps ship on his way to India.

His step-father wants to cure him of 'literature'.
Once a poet makes his mark, no tide can wash away
his words: '*Au pays parfumé que le soleil caresse*'.
And what can I say, he was so delicious!

Sadly sweet Baudelaire soon finds himself
in such a profound melancholy,
after seeing a whipping in the main square,
after two weeks, he sails to France, leaving me

a sonnet. With the pride and jealousy of
the British Admiralty she punishes me
with her passion for corsets, sea-blockades
and endless petticoats wide as the Empire.

The oldest profession is alive and thrives
in my harbours; strumpets and exports, cross-
dressing captains and girls in white breeches.
Boys who like boys who like collars and chains.

She brings a pantomime cast of *malabars*
and *lascars* to my shores. Their passage back
to India guaranteed, if only they can read the scripts.
The cane breaks backs. Tamil, Urdu, Hindi, cling

to their skins like beads of sweat. Hundreds of
    tongues
parched like the mouths of sweet-hearts in an arranged
ceremony. She is kind and ruthless and insists
on the Queen's English. At night Creole verve slips in

and makes mischief. Each time she comes she
    pretends
it's the first time she has landed here, but she soon
becomes bored. Tired of flogging and kicking
the dogs. She doesn't know which uniform to wear.

'I'm no one and everyone', she complains.
'And you have no more distinguishing marks
left to conquer'. She pulls down her Union
Jack; it falls like a sari, around her bare feet.

*Marrons*: Creole name given to the slaves taken from
Madagascar and transported convicts.
*Malabars and Lascars*: Hindu and Muslim indentured
  labourers.
These names are disparaging terms in Mauritian Creole.

## Sea patois

We had gestures, upside down feet, signals,
our bubbles crested into sea ash, our salt cooked
into yellow. We sheltered in a gasp,
a slip of dream. Our legs kicked out of sync,
interrupting the ocean's thoughts of fire-birds.

We were sunk, passed through amber and incense,
our lungs expanded starboard. We were burnt,
scattered backwards like unrefined sugar, our spirits
riding the deep pressure swells. Choked
on our own turquoise, we swallowed the horizon

and woke the half-eyed sun. Our love never
reached land, never discovered the New World
had weak ankles, tendons of dried seaweed.

# 'Bringing the Head and the Body Together'

## VALERIE MASON-JOHN AND DOROTHEA SMARTT IN CONVERSATION

*Maggie Gee*

*Valerie Mason-John began her writing career as an international correspondent covering Aboriginal Land Rights in Australia. In 2000, she won the Windrush Achievement Award for services to the British Black Community. She is co-author and editor of the only two books to document the lives of African and Asian lesbians in Britain,* Making Black Waves (1993) and Talking Black: Lesbians of African and Asian Descent Speak Out (1994), *as well as* Brown Girl in the Ring: Plays, Prose and Poems (1998). *She was artistic director of the Pride and London Mardi Gras Arts Festivals. In 2005 she published her debut novel,* Borrowed Body, *which won the inaugural Shorelines and Culture Word Prize before publication and the MIND Book Award in 2006. Her most recent book,* Detox Your Heart, *is a self-help book about dealing with anger, and she is currently working on a new novel about the Dalit communities of India, entitled* A Corrupted Gene. *She is ordained into the Western Buddhist Order and lives in England and the USA.*

*Dorothea Smartt is a British-born poet and artist of Barbadian or 'Bajan' heritage who has received critical acclaim in Europe, the Caribbean and the USA. She was Brixton Market's first Poet-in-Residence, and an Attached Live Artist at London's Institute of Contemporary Arts (ICA). Her poetry collection* Connecting Medium *was published by Peepal Tree Press in 2001. It contains a highly commended Forward Poetry Prize poem, and poems from her live art pieces* Medusa *and* From You To Me To You *(an ICA Live Arts commission). Most recently she has produced her first short films for her installation/performance* Just A Part, *commissioned by AFFORD (African Foundation for Development), and* Bringing It All Back Home, *inspired by Sambo's Grave on Sunderland Point (a Lancaster LitFest commission) and due to be published by Peepal Tree. She is* Sable Litmag's *poetry editor.*

**Maggie Gee** I would like to ask you both how you began.

**Valerie Mason-John** I learned that I loved writing when I did my 'A' Levels. I did English, Psychology and Economic and Social History — I wanted to be a historian. Two of my heroes were C L R James and E P Thompson and I actually saw them in conversation. I loved writing the essays. I didn't think I wanted to be a writer, but I had a passion for it.

**MG** And when did the journalism come?

**VMJ** I set up a magazine called *Jezebel* with some friends at Leeds University. It was just after the Yorkshire Ripper was caught in the 1980s, so it was a very intense time. Female students were given a minibus to go home in, there was a women's centre. I dropped out of university in the second year, came to London and started working as a volunteer on *Monochrome*, which had been the old *Leveller* and grew out of *The Guardian*. I covered the Broadwater Farm Riots etc and really enjoyed it, and ended up doing a post-graduate course in journalism.

**MG** Dorothea, when did you start writing poetry?

**Dorothea Smartt** I started in my late teens but I wasn't showing it to anybody — I was doing other writing that I showed to people. Valerie was involved with *Monochrome* and I was in the Brixton Black Women's Group and contributing to their newsletter, *Speak Out,* writing book reviews and reviews of performances. Prior to that I worked on the *London Women's Liberation Newsletter*. And just like Valerie, I had an interest in history, I had an 'A' Level in Psychology and I got really excited about Sociology. I saw writing as very much about women, and black people

*Wasafiri Vol. 22, No. 1 March 2007, pp. 14–20*
ISSN 0269-0055 print/ISSN 1747-1508 online © 2007 Maggie Gee
http://www.tandf.co.uk/journals    DOI: 10.1080/02690050601097567

especially, fulfilling a need to write our own stories because nobody was going to do it for us. I was writing poetry as well, but not thinking that much of it.

**MG** Not showing it to anyone?

**DS** No, it was just something that I did for me. And through working in radical bookshops, many that don't exist anymore, I got to find out about things like the International Book Fair of Radical Black and Third World Books and the feminist book fairs that used to happen. I went along and heard poetry performed and language used in ways that I hadn't before, and got really excited about that. I did get frustrated at school. I was a kid who read a lot, but I got to a point where I got concerned about what I was reading. I read Enid Blyton like everybody else, the *Malory Towers* books. And Barbara Cartland, I read endless, endless novels — for the history I told myself, it was a fun way of doing history. Then through the radical bookshops I got exposed to whole other areas of writing that I didn't know about.

**MG** What about poetry?

**DS** At school I read Keats and enjoyed delving into the layers of imagery, but if I think in terms of what influenced me, it would be songs. When I was about thirteen, my favourite album was Joni Mitchell's *Mingus* — I liked the words. I was living in Battersea, and you could borrow albums from the libraries. I was borrowing things that I used to think no one else would want to listen to — Bernie Taupin, you know. 'The Captain and the Kid', Elton John . . . it was about the lyrics.

**VMJ** I read Enid Blyton and *Malory Towers* too, I grew up in a kid's home so institutional books were great. But when I think of influences, I should say that Dorothea and I are exactly the same generation, and we're part of a renaissance. Dorothea was in Sistahs In Song, a black women's group who performed at a black women's centre. People were performing, and I remember feeling this urge to perform but felt like I couldn't do anything because it all seemed a bit Afrekeke — a bit kind of Caribbean-based or Black British . . .

**MG** Why would that be a problem?

**VMJ** Because I grew up in a white context, I didn't have that language at that point. I came to London and everybody told me that I was too white. Two people who really empowered me though were Jackie Kay and Lorna Leslie. When I heard Jackie Kay performing, it was like wow! She was speaking in a Scottish vernacular, she had a language and she really spoke to me. And somebody who Dorothea lived with, Lorna Leslie. There were a couple of black women's exhibitions at Brixton Art Gallery, and Lorna said 'You're a writer, go and write some poetry'. The two poems I wrote got mentioned by *City Limits*. Coming back to the books that inspired me, I have to say

Thomas Hardy's *Return of the Native* and E M Forster's *Passage to India*.

**MG** Was it novels rather than poetry?

**VMJ** Yes. And Barbara Burford's short story 'The Threshing Floor', which had a black character in it who grew up in a kid's home who was a dyke and I thought, ah, somebody writing about me. I did read poetry at school, and I always used to love those things 'Love is . . .', in graffiti phrases. But really, poetry wasn't just on the paper, it was performance. Being a journalist, I did get the luxury of going to performances. And there was Bernardine Evaristo and the Theatre of Black Women, so I was really well-fed from a performance point of view.

**DS** You've just reminded me — I started working at Sister Write bookshop and was studying at South Bank Polytechnic and was able to access people like Nella Larsen and Zora Neale Hurston. Valerie mentioned the Theatre of Black Women. I think the first review that I ever wrote for *Spare Rib* was of Theatre of Black Women. I had gone to Amsterdam to a women's festival, and was totally amazed and inspired by Bernardine Evaristo and Patricia Saint Hilaire. They were just starting out with the theatre company together. I was inspired by Jackie Kay as well. She was one of the few black women that I knew who, if you asked her what she did, said that she was a writer and a poet.

**VMJ** I've only just started calling myself a writer.

**DS** I was really impressed by that and wondered how she dared to do it. I remember at Sister Write one of the things I saw as part of my job was to ensure that there was good representation of black writers. And the good thing about the Black Radical International Book Fair was being exposed to Caribbean writers. I was studying the Harlem Renaissance, finding out about the black arts movement in the US in the 1960s, and reading people like Nikki Giovanni. This was in the early eighties, and I was living on Nursery Road, and Valerie lived across the street.

**MG** How hard was it to start performing? Were you performing publicly in spaces that were identified as gay?

**VMJ** Well I performed at lesbian or gay events but that wouldn't be difficult because they were marketed to a lesbian and gay audience. But I also performed out there in the wider market, and I don't think I was billed as a lesbian. I trained in mime and physical theatre for fifteen months at the Desmond Jones School and that was brilliant. I learned to perform and to tell stories. I wrote my first book during that time, *Making Black Waves*, which was the first book to document the lives of African and Asian women in Britain.

**MG** Did you get adverse reactions from some Black British people?

**VMJ** Well, I was initially seen as a leading black female journalist, giving talks with people like John Pilger and Stuart Hood. I've still got the letter about interviewing Margaret Thatcher — it would have been the first time she had spoken to black media, but she backed out.

**MG** How about your 'Queenie' persona?

**VMJ** Well the performer came after the journalist, you see. After I got disillusioned with journalism, I re-trained. Where Queenie came from was — I realised that because I had been this hardcore journalist writing mainly for *The Voice* but also for *The Guardian*, freelance, if I then wanted to be this performer, how could I be Valerie Mason-John and do this flippant stuff? I had been named 'Queenie' in San Francisco, so people could make this shift with Queenie. I knew that it would be short-lived, but I loved performing. I wouldn't say that I performed lesbian stuff; that Queenie persona really came out of my piece on the Queen of England, where I mixed fact with fiction. *Brown Girl in the Ring*, the title of my third book, was also the title of the show I did which exposes the African origins of a European royal family. That's where that persona came from, and people loved it.

**MG** Dorothea, you ran and performed in the Word Up Women's Café performance space, and you also edited *Words from the Women's Café: Lesbian Poetry from Word Up*. How difficult was that?

**DS** I didn't meet any prejudice or cussing or anything like that because I was performing in women's spaces. And I wasn't performing overtly as a lesbian, at least I don't think I was. So I found those safe spaces to try out my first performance legs, and when I did read in more mixed settings,

I didn't necessarily read overtly lesbian stuff. At that point just being out as a feminist was enough of an issue, and the two words for some people were synonymous anyway. I don't have any formal training as such, I think the performing that I do I owe to the women around me. I was not only inspired by African American artists who would come over and visit but also by women around me in Brixton. It was a very exciting time in the mid stretch of eighties, I did my first art performance with a group of women, and Valerie was in it. And I was singing a cappella with Sistahs In Song at women's events and festivals. It was very much like a nursery, that space, but it's a continual process, moving out of there into new spaces that again would challenge my confidence about writing. It's not about arriving at a plateau and saying I'm there.

**VMJ** When I went out to a conference in Washington this year looking at the Black British Aesthetic, what was so fascinating to me was that the people they named were all hanging out with us, people like Lubaina Himid, Maud Salter, Ingrid Pollard, Dorothea and me.

**MG** So I guess my question about prejudice isn't relevant.

**VMJ** Well it was for me. It wasn't an issue in my social life because everything was done in the women's scene. But actually when Dorothea and I wrote an article together for *Spare Rib*, we had this argument because I didn't want to be identified as a feminist. As Dorothea says, being identified as feminist was synonymous with being a lesbian, and I had a reputation and didn't want people to know that. You know it's funny. I was worried about that, and yet I said yes when I was asked to write a book on lesbian stuff, *Making Black Waves*, because I thought it was important. I don't know where I was at. And the street we lived on, Nursery Road, was called 'Lesbian Street', it was full of black and white lesbians.

**DS** Not exclusively, but there was enough of us there —

**MG** To feel supported?

**DS** Yes.

**VMJ** Sixty percent of that street. And if you weren't a lesbian you were a gay guy or an artist. But then it got to a point when that started to fragment. All of the infrastructure started to dismantle. Then it was like oh, so I had done this lesbian stuff and started to create this body of work... It became an issue as I got older when I didn't have that infrastructure to hide behind.

**MG** You had been a real pioneer, though, with *Making Black Waves*, and in the prose commentary that frames the two plays in *Brown Girl in the Ring*, you wrote stunningly directly and honestly about your own 'awakening to lesbianism'. You also gave a fascinating cultural history of how the lives of black and

Asian lesbians evolved over the last two decades or so. But at the end of that book you wrote that however attached you were to your 'lesbian self, black self, female self', you also felt bigger than those identities or labels, and sometimes wanted to 'become a Buddhist nun and lead a spiritual life'. What do you feel now, eight years later? How does it affect your writing?

**VMJ** *Brown Girl in the Ring* was the end of an era for me — the end of my being so identified with my sexuality. It was my third book, and I wanted to document some of my work which hadn't been published, and also to talk about black lesbian culture without feeling censored by the community. Because the first two books were the only ones in this country on African and Asian lesbian culture, it was important to reflect as many voices as possible, but the third book was my voice only. In 2004 I was ordained in to the Western Buddhist Order in India, so my desire to live more wholeheartedly as a Buddhist has been fulfilled. My writing has changed, my novel reflects some Buddhist theories on rebirth, and my most recent book, *Detox Your Heart,* works with anger, fear and hatred. This is at the heart of Buddhism, working with our suffering, purifying our hearts. Being a nun? I'm not sure about that one — I'm thinking of adopting a child — but who knows what will happen in my life.

**MG** Dorothea, can labels get in the way?

**DS** I don't think I ever set out to be a black lesbian writer. If I wanted a label I would be more open to being identified as a black woman writer. In the 1980s I defined myself as a black socialist feminist, but within that and within black politics, I was interested in black women writers and creative expression.

**MG** The British literary establishment has not been particularly welcoming to black women writers.

**DS** No, but there have been times in my life when I wasn't looking to the dominant white male literary establishment for understanding or critical appreciation. Because I didn't think that they were about to give it.

**VMJ** As a writer, critics have put labels on me, it's not that I've put labels on myself. When I've stepped out of writing what's perceived to be black or lesbian, that's when they've tried to box me in. It happened with my show *Brown Girl in the Ring*. At first none of the media wanted to touch it because they couldn't believe that Queen Victoria had African ancestry — Queen Charlotte, who was married to King George IV. Then *The Sunday Times* did this article saying that I was right, but they called me a 'political activist'. I wrote to them and asked, if I was white would I be called a political activist? I'm a writer. There's a book, *Alternatives in the Mainstream: Black and Asian Theatre*. The writer, Dimple Godiwala, has done a critique of the play *Brown Girl in the Ring* and called it lesbian . . . Actually there's nothing to do with lesbian sexuality in that

© R E Griffiths

play but, because I'm a dyke, people think there has to be. I live in a predominantly white heterosexual world, and I should be able to write about other stuff. My training as a journalist has allowed me to write about everything. I just write about what I'm passionate about.

**MG** Dorothea, can you tell us something about the complex and subtle Medusa sequence in your collection of poetry, *Connecting Medium*?

**DS** *Connecting Medium* came after a very, very long process, after many different performances and performance pieces. I developed the Medusa piece when I was at Hunter College in the US in the mid-eighties studying Anthropology, but also looking at literature as a form of cultural expression; also at migration, identity and ethnicity and using that to explore my own Caribbean heritage.

**MG** For performance?

**DS** No, I was just 'doing' them, they just came out of my mouth. One of the ways I write is as though I'm talking to myself, almost dictating. I'm not thinking about it on the page but getting down something that's in my head. And that's what happened with the Medusa poems. I was looking at black aesthetics and what was acceptable in terms of black hair and things like that. That's when I started wearing dreadlocks, and I wore them for about eighteen years. So I did the Medusa piece and the voice for it was very Bajan, what I'd call my first voice. It was the way that I had learned to speak English from my parents, but school attempted to rob me of that voice. I made a conscious decision in my late teens to hold on to it, through discovering writers like Kamau Brathwaite and the African Caribbean writer Paule Marshall. Her book, *Brown Girl Brownstones*, is a coming-of-age story of a young African American girl who grows up in a Caribbean household. So she has to deal with the world inside her home where her mum spoke this particular way, and the different world outside.

**MG** You've said that poetry saved your primary voice, your Bajan voice, Caribbean voice.

**DS** Well, I started using it in my everyday life. Because of that particular way of writing, that almost dictating to myself. I was influenced as well by people who had nothing to do with writing, by song and voice — Ingrid Pollard, Sonia Boyce, Keith Piper. All this amazing stuff was happening in black visual arts. I have always been interested in visuals as well and the Medusa piece was where I first bought visuals together with my words. And it was selected by a guest programmer at the ICA as part of a season of lesbian and gay live art. That was a critical point in my development as an artist. The cycle of Medusa poems and visuals were very important to me, speaking as they do of the politics and aesthetics of black women's appearance. That ICA season, entitled *It's Not Unusual*, led to my becoming Attached Live Artist there and helped to develop my live art work through working with the Black Arts Alliance, a Manchester-based national organisation that supports black live arts.

**MG** Valerie, I want to ask you about voice. One of the things that you write about very interestingly in *Borrowed Body* is the experience of Pauline, who is perceived to be posh and white and not properly black. The child's voice is very believable. And then there's the narrating voice in your non-fiction book about dealing with anger, *Detox Your Heart,* a very kind, wise voice. I know it's not primarily meant as a literary book, but there are some beautiful sentences, like 'The sky is free and there is enough for everybody'. When you write, do you 'hear' your writing?

**VMJ** I hear voice when I write, I'm very much in the characters. *Brown Girl in the Ring* was so liberating for me because I found one of my voices and it connected to both black and white people.

**MG** Describe that voice.

**VMJ** The voice is a white middle-class voice and I know it because I grew up around it, almost from the moment I was born. I came to creole voice when I was about eleven or twelve and Black English at the same time, these new voices. Voice fascinates me. In my new novel, although there is a bit of Black English in there with some characters, I feel as though I am writing mainly with an English voice, my first voice. One family is very middle class, moneyed, and the other family is also middle class but not moneyed. I have several voices. And the work that I do also really informs my voice — working with young people.

**MG** Is this the anger management training that you do?

**VMJ** Yes, I'm working with homeless street people, which is why I feel that I was able to get that particular voice in *Borrowed Body*.

**DS** I feel that I have several voices too. In some ways that middle-class English voice is as much part of the Caribbean heritage as patois and creole and the nation languages. I grew up in working-class Battersea and I have a voice that's a particular working-class voice from there. But then there's also the voice that came through my education.

**MG** Do you think it helps you, having this range of voices?

**DS** Most people have a range of voices. It's just about how legitimate you think they are, and how confident you are about using them. As an artist I want to write about, and perform about, anything I choose to. If I choose to look at slavery I do it because I want to do it, because it is a topic that I as a black woman, a Black British writer, want to be exploring. I needed to explore my Caribbean voice at a particular point in my life, but it's not my only voice and there have been times when I didn't want to get pigeon-holed or trapped in it.

**VMJ** When I came to London I needed to find a black voice to survive in the communities that I was in. Without it my life was hell, it really was. I needed to be able to seen as one of them. And what happened, and what was really hard, was that I denied my white voice because of that, I shut it out and in a way that kind of blocked me. And it's only been in the past six years that I can say yes, this is a part of me, let me embrace it. I know my black self now, I needed to discover it, but actually a part of me is my white self. When you're trans-racially placed through fostering and children's homes, as I was, it's not that you're mixed race, but you do have a mixed culture. I didn't have a black culture, so it's been imperative to find all my voices and not deny any of them because of society. A lot of people have that need. There's also the voice through education — if a person grows up in a very white working-class background, then has education, then comes back into the family, which voice do they use? When I'm working with writers I ask them 'What is your voice?' So they're not just using borrowed voices.

**MG** Dorothea, I noticed, reading the two versions of the title poem of your collection *Connecting Medium*, one written in 1993 and the other in 2001, how much you re-write, the extent to which all your poems are carefully worked. You've credited Kwame Dawes's Afro-style School with making you aware of form.

**DS** The Afro-style School was an initiative of Spread the Word. They set up master classes for generations of black poets. I was at a point where I was more open to exploring forms and also curious to see what forms might be innate in my own work. I found reading Patience Agbabi inspiring, because of how she would use form, but it wasn't something

I felt confident to do. Then I found inspiration in Kwame's workshops. What was important to me was his own grounding in African, African Caribbean and African American literatures, and his interest and curiosity about Black British literatures.

**MG** How many times do you revise a poem?

**DS** It varies. I'm not always very patient. It can go on for a number of years on and off. And I think that it's important for my process just to let things sit.

**MG** So you go away and leave it?

**DS** Yes, and then I come back to it and it's clearer. Or I might scrap it altogether. Putting a book together made me much more self-conscious. And working with Kwame Dawes, Jacob Ross and Bernardine Evaristo, as well, made me much more careful about writing something that worked on the page. Most of my work starts out as things I intend to perform, and then when I start to think about publishing them, that's when they get re-worked, as much as ten times. I don't know if it ever stops, because sometimes when I'm reading poems from *Connecting Medium*, I'm still fiddling with them.

**MG** *Connecting Medium* is beautifully structured, it works as a kind of very delicate dance with your life. It's not exactly chronological but you take us back through the ancestors and the parents in 1950s Britain and then you look at love and you have this theme of yearning for America, and travel, and political things about black hair and so on. And then you move to this mythical writing. So you open out from the personal to the universal. I wonder how much work that was.

**DS** A lot of work. I found it really hard to sequence the poems and there were about four or five drafts of that manuscript. Still not feeling that it was right, I then got saved by a wonderful editor, Jeremy Poynting.

**MG** Valerie, *Borrowed Body* went through long years of editing. You were working on the draft of it for your MA, I think. Can you say something about form?

**VMJ** My first love is poetry. I learned about form through poetry. It was fantastic for me that Peter Abbs was teaching at Sussex, and he's a brilliant poet. And in my second year, I was very fortunate to have Catherine Smith, one of the 2005 'New Generation' poets. Some of that first draft of the book was in the collection of poetry that I put together for the MA.

**DS** Some of the best novelists are good poets too.

**VMJ** Also, as Dorothea says, it's important to sit with it. In a way I wish that I had had more time to sit with it, I've learned that I don't have to rush, there's no train to catch. When a book comes out, it comes out. But form — I suppose I wasn't really aware of form as I was writing it, I just knew that it was a

linear story. I'm an intuitive writer and that's how I work, something emerges and I will go there. The form and the crafting happens in the rewriting, and that's what I enjoy. Once I've got a reasonable first draft together, I send it out to a few people to get their feedback and then take it to another draft, leave it, take it to another draft, leave it ...

**MG** The book is very carefully worked. I mean the pace, the voice, but also the way you intercut between realism and passages where the spirits enter the story, Sparky, Arabella, Snake and, most interestingly of all, the African chief with the gold.

**VMJ** When I was very young, my house parents used to do a ouija board after we went to bed, so I knew about poltergeists. And my mum did *obeah*. So both from a white European's perspective and from an African perspective, I was open to the spirit worlds.

**MG** It's very interesting and mysterious, the way you use the spirit figure of the African chief. Pauline herself doesn't understand why he appears or where he comes from. Only at the end does this figure start to really take on significance because you tell us he is a chief who has sold most of the village into slavery, and Pauline, at a climactic point, says sorry on his behalf.

**VMJ** I was working with the idea that there were African people who did sell slaves. The book opens with a spirit wanting to come back into the world, so I'm working with past lives and karma. Because the spirit was in a rush to be born, it made a mistake.

**MG** And got the wrong mother. A cruel mother.

**VMJ** Yes. But why did the spirit choose this person to be born to? The connection was in past life. Pauline's mother was the chief's wife.

**MG** 'My mother my wife', Pauline says. So Pauline was once that African chief? Is that why she says sorry?

**VMJ** Yes. So it's playing with that idea of re-birth and past lives.

**MG** Dorothea, Medusa, the snake-haired Gorgon, is an incredible image and the way you use it is so powerful. We know in classical mythology that using the mirror to look at the Gorgon is the only safe way to do it, but in your poem the mirror can turn the world's view of Medusa back on herself — you're talking about hair, and you say 'turn it back on itself'.

**DS** I was literally thinking about the fact that, as people with African hair, our hair curls in a particular direction, it has a natural kink. So then we straighten it and curl it in a 'proper' kink. There's something supposedly wrong with the natural curl, so we have to undo it and curl it back on itself. But I was also concerned with internalisation, turning things back on ourselves, and seeing ourselves through that particular lens. I only had Perseus' word for it that Medusa was an ugly monster. If the only press that Medusa ever read of herself was what Perseus wrote … There's the whole idea that black women are ugly, we're too dark, we're too this and too that. Who says we are? What aesthetic reference are you using that allows us to become ugly or exoticised, or physical curios? When I was locksing up my hair, I was struck by how it changed peoples' reactions to me. So there are lots of ways I can relate to Medusa. I think that her killing was quite cowardly, because Perseus, the 'hero' of the story, never actually looks his enemy in the eye, he just looks at the reflection of her in a mirror. It's as though you only deal with society's reflection of you.

**MG** In one version of the story, Athene, Goddess of Wisdom and Knowing, asked Perseus for Medusa's head, because Medusa had claimed to be more beautiful than her. So it might never have been true that Medusa was ugly.

**DS** I studied the sociology of knowledge, who decides what is and isn't valid. Legitimate forms of knowledge and legitimate ways of knowing. And I guess I took that with me in thinking about Medusa.

**MG** One poem that I find almost unbearably powerful is 'Medusa Dream'. The image stays with me of Medusa's head, at the end of the poem, looking down at the body, and the body is lying on the floor. And it's such a visceral, gut-wrenching image. I am interested in this whole body-head separation thing.

**DS** When I was writing that poem there was that sense it was based on dreams. That idea of being woken up from sleep and not being in your body — that split second sensation. In some myths, Perseus kills Medusa in her sleep. But as you realise you're looking at your body you go back into it. You need balance, you need to be able to bring the head and the body together.

One way of dealing with our history as black people – the violence and brutality – is to rationalise and intellectualise it, rather than experiencing the hurt. Our genetic memory of hurt might drive us to live in our heads. Aspects of our history, we can deal with it in an intellectual way, but there is also the madness and the terror — the moment before you catch the light at the end of the tunnel, a moment of hopelessness, like in my poem 'The Middle Passage', the moment when it's totally dark.

**VMJ** With the character of Pauline, my intention was to show what happened to children with dysfunction — their survival mechanism is splitting. Adults do it with alcohol, kids do it at a psychological level. They leave their body because it is unbearable to be in their body. In another sense, you have to be prepared to go out of your body as a writer, to go to those places of madness.

The split between head and heart is a theme of *Detox Your Heart*. Eastern thought doesn't split head and heart, Western does. We try and think away the feelings. But as writers, there is a process of integration — at the end it is all woven together.

**MG** Thank you both for talking so generously.

# Suniti Namjoshi

*Sycorax*

## 1 Prologue

Old women do not die easily, nor
are their deaths timely. They make a habit
of outliving men, so that, as I'm still here,
I'm able to say clearly that when Prospero
said he took over an uninhabited island
save for Caliban and the enslaved
Ariel, he lied.
    I LIVED ON THAT ISLAND.
It was my property (at least as much
as it was anybody else's). He
drove me away, made himself king, set up
his props and bided his time.
    Now that they've gone
I may return, and ask myself, not who
they were, but who I was and what I mourn.
There's greenery left, a clear stream or two,
and Ariel, perhaps, checking his reflection
in yet another pool. Caliban's gone,
went with the gods who were only men. It's
what he deserves. He wanted so much
to be just like them.
    What is my task?
Because they've gone, must I go too? Take leave
of my senses one by one, or two by two?

*The good witch Sycorax has bright blue eyes*
*and now she's on her own she may fantasise.*

## 2 Animals

What can I say
    when the island recedes
and the dog has her day?

Is the dog real or unreal?
Which bitch is this
    come to disturb my final bliss?

It's necessary to distinguish between unreal animals and real ones. First there's the bitch. I am not afraid of her. She does not bite. But I do not like her. One day she will come up to me and lick me all over while looking at me with sad mocking eyes. To be so spiteful and so reproachful all at the same time! And about what? What did I ever do? That is the problem.

The real animals are easier to deal with. A lizard for instance. I could catch a lizard and sink my teeth in. Yes, I've eaten her raw. Not pretty, but matter of fact. I need to live. The lizard, of course, is forced to die. No malice there. Is that my excuse? Real animals are not symbolic. They do not mean anything. And that too is a lie.

It's a useful distinction. Sometimes though it's hard to tell what is real — in a dream, for instance, composed of something that happened, or might very well have happened. That's where those badger-like animals live. They always appear when somebody dies. They raise their bloodied snouts to the sky and they mourn. They frighten me most, because, I suppose, I recognise them.

There are birds on this island — sparrows,
well, a solitary sparrow. I admire
the patterns on her back. So subtle, I think.
(When sparrows were many, I didn't think that.)
I speak to the sparrow. I twitter at her!
But the sparrow is fighting final
extinction. Perhaps she thinks I'm comical?
Perhaps she thinks she is tragical? She says
she only wants to know if I have food
for her. If not, she'll look somewhere else.

Once I wanted to learn the language of birds, of all sorts of animals, even pigs, but most especially birds. Oh I fancied

*Wasafiri Vol. 22, No. 1 March 2007, pp. 21–25*
ISSN 0269-0055 print/ISSN 1747-1508 online © 2007 Suniti Namjoshi
http://www.tandf.co.uk/journals    DOI: 10.1080/02690050601097765

myself chattering with birds! I spent the rest of my life
unlearning that. Now when pigs scream and chickens stutter,
I hear nothing, nothing at all that makes any sense.

On this island though, I may dream again. On this island,
where the earth is waiting to eat me up, I know very well —
whether or not the birds and beasts acknowledge it — that I am
one of them.

> So that? If anything monstrous happened,
>     someone could dream in the wild wood.
> And all that had happened be rehearsed
>     until at last it was understood.

## 3 Physicality

> Berries slip through my hand
>     and roll on the ground.
> Can I bend and pick them up?
>     Will my back crack?
> Matters of physicality
>     achieve importance.

I am the old woman who lived in a shoe who had so many
children she didn't know what to do because they were all
starving to death. I am Old Mother Hubbard, who lived in a
cupboard, who couldn't give her dog a bone, because she
needed it for soup and had gnawed on it herself. Strange, just
as the flesh is loosening its grip, problems of survival manifest
themselves.

## 4 Copies

> One day my mind malfunctioned.
>     It made copy after copy
>         of me as I am,
> so I kicked my mind.
>     It then produced copies
>         distanced in time.
> It said to me, 'You may speak
>     to the good witch Syco
>         at the age of five.'

> Blue-eyed and blonde —
>     who would not love
> this sweet child?
>     We played for a while.
> 'Tell me,' I murmured,
>     'Did you really believe
>         you were really loved
>             at the age of five?'
> Her face altered.
>     'I believed what I liked!'
>         I nodded.
> Here I was, living proof
>     that she had survived.

It's not much fun meeting copies of earlier selves. One
knows what they know. And their stunned disbelief when they
look at one is not always flattering. But the other day, that
erratic computer, my meandering mind, produced a copy of my
mother: Syco the Dam, also blonde, also blue-eyed, but twenty
years older, and also engaged in taking leave of her senses. I
asked her — I asked her something . . . Perhaps I asked — But
it's no use, her hearing was the first to go. She hears voices, of
course. Always has done.

## 5 Ariel

I've decided that Ariel is a type of gay man, eternally
preoccupied, and endlessly young. He could go away if he
liked and look for company, but who would he find as
beautiful as he? And who would I find as interesting as me? In
consequence we do not speak to each other.

*It's clear that the old woman is as bad as the old man.
There is no difference in their indifference. She thinks I'm as
cold as water or as harsh as stone — in accordance with her
mood. She does not know that in trying to please I have
forgotten who I am. She sees only that I'm probably not who
she wants me to be.*

> Ariel turns his back on me.
>     I, mine, on him.
> One day I will die. (Ariel,
>     I suppose, is dead
> already.) He will not grieve.
> But the trees will grieve,
>     the leaves might grieve
> In their own way they might
>     sense a difference
> in the light and shade, an absence
>     rather than a presence,
> and Ariel in his pine tree, or oak tree,
>     or whichever tree
> it happens to be, will wail tunelessly.

*My singing is not tuneless! And anyway it's better than her
dancing. I've seen her frolicking: clasping the fog to her bosom
like a young girl or pretending to dodge between raindrops
like a happy child. I've heard her singing: that the weather is
her playmate, that the lightning offers ribbons for her hair, that
the function of thunder is to accompany her voice. She is a very
foolish old woman. Doesn't she realise that I am the weather?
Sometimes I think I'm the mud underfoot, that I am the island.
Well, I might be.*

Ariel is trying to frighten me. As though I, Syco, who have
seen the world and been through so much, could ever be fearful.
(The trouble is having seen the world and been through so much
does make one fearful.) This morning the sun rose. That was not
Ariel's doing. How could it be? And a sick rose bloomed outside
my window. Ariel made it sick? But it's autumn. Winter is
approaching. And I trod on a snail. Ariel made me! That's
absurd. I'm becoming paranoid. That is Ariel's doing! He has
done it so that then he might matter to me.

*The spiteful old thing! She created a storm to drown my singing. And yesterday, as I was drifting through the air minding my own business, she made a cliff face rise in front of me. I am going to disguise myself and spy on her so that I'll always know exactly where she is.*

Ariel has become a bird. If he could have contented himself with something muted, he could have been the sparrow's companion. But to turn himself into a bright red bird, a cardinal, no less?! He knows very well there are no cardinals on this island, all of which raises an ontological question: if Ariel exists, but cardinals do not, then is Ariel metamorphosed an unreal bird or a real one? Being followed about by a red bird with a two note whistle, going *fee fee* every two minutes, makes me ridiculous, though I don't think he whistles to annoy me. I think he does it for verisimilitude.

## 6 The Old Woman's Secrets

### The First Secret

*She is lonely.*

The good witch Sycorax with streaming eyes
has left herself with empty sockets.
Their blueness has dissolved in water,
and she sits like an idol on her lonely
island, wishing that someone would come.
They would give her sapphires for eyes.
                              But nobody comes.

### The Second Secret

*She talks to herself*

Blue was always my colour, my blue eyes were my one claim to fame. But as I've walked through the world what I've seen around me is red and green. Even on this island, which is deserted, there's red and green. But it's muted. I can ignore it. Things grow — that's green. Things die — that's red. But here, the glass green blades do not necessarily cut my feet, and I can avoid seeing my own blood shed. Other creatures scurry through the undergrowth. Some are caught. Blood is shed. But if I try hard I can avoid thinking about it. After all, the death of a gnat is hardly a cataclysmic event. So then? Is the importance of a life commensurate with the noise it makes? I am not going quietly into that good night, am I? It is the senselessness of it of it I've never understood.

### The Third Secret

*She is self critical.*

Now there is nothing to offer.
Now there is nowhere to go.
The old woman weeps on her island.
This accomplishes nothing,
does not water the seedlings,
does not make the potatoes grow.

A few must have known it was all red and green,
    but there I was with my blue streak of folly,
                    reaching for the skies.

### And the Fourth Secret

*At night she turns into a witch.*

Like anyone else old women metamorphose
at night. They drift like owls not knowing what
dreams they might light upon, nor whom they
        might
meet. Sometimes they sleep like kingfishers
on the charmèd wave and wake so refreshed
that when they look about them, they truly
        believe
that they have the power to control themselves
and the sea. Or they slip like seals through
        black
water from island to island and choose their
        dreams:
they're rich and powerful, or, sometimes, merely
        happy.
Old women do not desire desire. Behind
their eyes the sky burns a ferocious blue
and their skulls are lit by the sun's energy.

## 7 Visitors

In the quiet evening visitors come.
Birds fly, fish swim,
and even my fellow human beings
have their various modes of travel.
All are not always unwelcome.

The bat says to me: 'I am rare.
            I am precious,
though not necessarily beautiful.'
        'What did it cost?'
'Almost certain extinction.'

The dolphin has a different tale:
                        'They think
that because my mouth curves upwards

and I leap into the air, I do not feel
the slightest pain, that I am not capable of
being murderous.
                    Ludicrous!
                            Them, not me.
They are both murderous and ludicrous:
an unpleasant mix,
                    and hard to turn into literature.'

While the lizard claims I do not have the right
to welcome her. This is her home, her shack,
and her planet. Her ancestors preceded mine.

As for Sparrow, she's too ill
to know who or what or where she is,
and that she ought, perhaps, to make an effort.

And then one morning Ariel's twin
wanders in.
            She is charming,
though there is a resemblance.
            All day long
she defers to me. She says
                    she was passing by,
passing through.
            Ariel perhaps
in a fleeting mood, being at last
            who I'd like her to be?

In the late evening everyone leaves
and everything hurts. The only caresses
are from shadows gliding over my skin.

## 8 For that one thing

I look for the things I used to know.
The hill still slopes, the stream
flows. My tumbledown shack
                    has tumbled down,
and Prospero's shack
                    is bare and empty.
What he said and thought
                    is written down.
But what did he mean?
                    What was it I did?
That one thing? 'For which they would not
take my life'?
            That I had Caliban?
Were it not for the children, we'd be
two different species vying for precedence.
And yet,
            they disliked Caliban.

What was it then?
                    A chance smile?
The colour of my hair?
            The excellence of my intellect?
Whatever it was,
            it was inadvertent.

## 9 Being Robbed

The old man robbed me. With age
and envy he had grown into a hoop,
but he was not my real enemy.

The real enemy rides in the sea wave,
hides in the foam, seduces with jasmine,
and clutches at my robes with the tiniest of demands
like the briars on a rose, and is here, there
and everywhere, and is not Ariel.
                            Ariel
is only a copy of a dream.
                    But the enemy
devours me daily and I let him, because
in this one matter I am unable
to exercise my will.
One day he tarnished my eyesight.
                            Why tarnish
my eyesight, when I so admired him?
One day he deafened me.
                    And this
just after I had heard him sing.
One day he robbed me
                of Caliban and the island.
And one day he will take everything.

## 10 By the wayside

Syco sits by the wayside mourning her death. Seeing a passer-by, she calls out to him, 'Hey! Gimme a word? Two or three words, an entire epitaph?' But the passer-by does what they always do, so she scratches about and writes her own poem.

   The next day she scours the seashore. She finds a whole shoal of fish rolling in the waves, she yells out to them, 'Oi! If you've got a minute, could you listen to my poem?' They stand on their tails, and listen politely. When she's done, they disperse noisily. She has no way of knowing if they liked her poem.

   The following day she climbs a tree. She has a bagful of chips to entice seagulls. They need no enticing. They dive at her. She fights back. She dictates terms: one chip per poem which she'll inscribe on their backs. The gulls decline. She hadn't realised they set such store by their dapper image. She lowers her sights and makes a deal with the sparrow, who summons other sparrows: one chip per word, and one word per sparrow. It's all they can take, the sparrows explain, anything more is beyond their strength. Her poem's fragmented. It doesn't matter. In her head dedicated sparrows swoop and swerve and swerve again forever and ever against a blue sky.

## 11 Timelessness you know

As death approaches thieves walk
                                    on cold water
and the nightmares never cease.

                                    Timelessness
you know. The broken mind — broken
                              you know.
Off the time track — swishing about
                              in a pool of time.

There are natterings and whispers.
The heirs have departed,
   but nevertheless whispers:
what do you bequeath to those who are living?
My name on the waters written in a richer,
deeper dye. My entire inheritance to those
who will keep my name from dissolving . . .
That was one day, but though the days
were falling fast, another thought
occurred on another day.
                  I leave you nothing.
I need it for myself.
                  Pray precede me.
I have no intention of just as yet dying.

Even so
         Death approached
at a snail's pace.
         Oh you foolish woman
(she said to herself),
         one day Achilles
will catch the tortoise.

## 12 The Death of Sycorax

Sycorax dissolves in the dew.
She dissolves in the foam,
   in the blue twilight,
leaving only a ripple on the waters,
   a mild turbulence
a not unpleasant odour.

She died in the morning with the lies
still swarming, the birds still singing,
the sun still rising —
                  all planetary preoccupations
as per normal —
and the Imperial Powers still warring.

When Sycorax died the island did not sink
                        into the ocean;
mud and rubble did not, at once,
                        dissolve in the sea;
            and nobody clapped.
The stage was left empty, till later,
                  somebody else occupied it.

## 13 Epilogue

O keep the blue wave from closing
                        over her head,
the foam from dissolving, the wind
from carrying all traces away.

# An Extract:
# *Illuminations* (1991)

**Maureen Duffy**

Illuminations *was written between the fall of the Berlin Wall and the first Gulf War. It was a moment of hope when it looked as if we might have learned something from the bloody history of the twentieth century with its devastating wars leading to the fall of three empires: Ottoman, British and Russian. The approaching millennium held out the promise of a new century that must surely be better. The love between Hetty and Helge, transcending the prejudices of sex, race, class, age and politics, embodies that hope. Sadly, fifteen years on, we haven't grown wiser. Gore Vidal's predicted new empire, global, corporate, economically all powerful, has renewed the old self interest, greed and tribalism. Even the hard-won freedom to enjoy and express love in all its rainbow colours is again under threat everywhere we look, except perhaps in the pages of this edition of* Wasafiri. – Maureen Duffy, October 2006.

The walk to the station reassures her a little. It's an autumn morning of gauzy sunlight with a faint smell of bonfires from suburban gardens where Michaelmas daisies are thrusting their lilac and blue banks between heavy-headed late roses that scatter blowsy petals on the neat patches of shorn grass. England seems caught in an eternal St Martin's summer before the two World Wars as Hetty goes downhill to the station where the Wandsworth crowds come up to meet her, urban and multicoloured, washing her along like tumbling shingle down the platforms, and pressing her among them into the train where some retreat into their own heads with paperbacks or earphones, plugging out the world while others rap as they strap-hang in the sing-song creole of cockney crossed with Caribbean, a code only penetrable by aficionados. These're more consciously natty than their white fellow travellers, Hetty decides. One young man who's alone stares straight ahead. His tall slim body in its fashionable baggy suit is topped by a polled head that has the bony elegance of Benin sculpture. An Asian girl further along the carriage has hair falling in skeins of black silk round a serenely beautiful coffee-cream face. Hetty feels blotchy and rubbed in her pink skin.

The lift at Russell Square Station is packed with its usual freight of tourists clutching maps in assorted languages. She's retracing the steps she used to take with Sandy when they came to inter-college lectures on Wednesday mornings to be carried away by M R Ridley sweeping them along with epic grandeur or Helen Gardner sugaring them with Elizabethan sonnets. Hetty turns left and crosses over Tavistock Street into the garden in the middle of the square where they had eaten their sandwiches on fine days. The same benches are there screened by dusty bushes behind the high iron railings but occupied by blear-eyed tramps talking in short broken phrases and nursing half-empty bottles. On one a boy in ragged dirty clothes is drawn up like a foetus on his side asleep. Hetty feels humiliated that these are the scenes of London life, like something from the pages of the Victorian Mayhew, that the tourists have to pass through. She crosses the little park diagonally, by paths flanked by beds of florid tea roses, coming out at the far corner opposite the side railings of the British Museum and makes her way past them until she can turn right, along the front to the main gates where the crowds throng in and out all day. She hasn't been here for years and it's much more populous than she remembers. Once it had seemed somehow privileged to come here at all. Now the hordes are cheerfully matter-of-fact and there are ice-cream vans and hotdog stands. Yet the Smirkes' great colonnaded portico is as impressive as she remembers and she can see among the groups of people waiting on the steps a figure she recognises (with relief because she had been afraid she wouldn't) as Helge Ebbesen, dressed like a student in blue jeans, white trainers and some sort of red shirt under a denim jacket. Hetty sees her scanning the advancing crowds and puts up a hand to wave. She's been seen; Helge waves back and

*Wasafiri Vol. 22, No. 1 March 2007, pp. 26–30*
ISSN 0269-0055 print/ISSN 1747-1508 online © 2007 Maureen Duffy
http://www.tandf.co.uk/journals    DOI: 10.1080/02690050601097575

Routledge
Taylor & Francis Group

begins to come down the wide stone steps towards her. She looks appallingly young.

'Hullo,' Hetty says. 'I hope you haven't been waiting long.'

'Not at all and it is such a beautiful day it doesn't matter. Where would you like to go. I hope you have a little time?'

'Oh I've lots of time. Maybe now we're here we could go inside. I haven't been for years. It must have changed so much.'

It has and yet it hasn't, Hetty decides quite quickly. The greatest change is the sheer number of people and the glass cage in the entrance hall with a crater full of money of all colours and denominations, an open begging bowl for Smirkes' shekels. But the temple itself, for that's what it is, is unchanged, the Assyrian sculptures as monumental as ever.

'We should look at the manuscripts perhaps?' Helge laughs. 'Or no, look we should visit our ancestors.'

'Our ancestors?'

'The Anglo-Saxons. There is a special exhibition.'

They climb the stairs and pass through Roman Britain, to the *Early Mediaeval Room*, past Merovingian, Slavic, Viking, Byzantium, the Lombards through Celtic and Germanic to the barbarian treasures of Raedwald, lost pagan King of East Anglia, sailing into the seas of the dead in his longboat with his Byzantine silver dinner service and Swedish armour, his lyre for singing Hel to sleep and his drinking horns for the eternal carousing to while away the night.

'It would be fun to live like that do you think?'

'Only if you were the King.'

'Now we should see the manuscripts?'

After the glitter of gold and sliver, enamel and semiprecious stones and green glass, the intricacy and variety of ivory, crystal inlay and engraving, the books seem at first subdued under the hushed lighting until, as their eyes become accustomed, they too begin to vibrate with colours and shapes while the elegant painstaking scripts assemble into lines and columns of meaning.

'Look here is the oldest piece of Saxon poetry. It says the letters show traces of Anglo-Saxon influence. *Heliond*: the Saviour. And it is here in London.'

'The spoils of Empire I expect. But then look here, it works both ways. The finest copy of this manuscript from Northumbria is in Italy.'

'But it says it was a present to the Pope.'

'These leaves had been used to bind an account book. There's a moral there.' But underneath Hetty is thinking that these were the kind of things Tetta looked at every day.

When they came into the sunshine again Hetty finds it hallucinatory in its brightness as if her eyes have been opened, from blind, and people, trees and buildings shimmer, dissolve and remake themselves in front of her.

'Have you time for some lunch?'

'Oh I think so. I'm quite hungry aren't you?'

But she isn't. Her heart seems to be permanently in her mouth and she feels a little sick and light-headed. 'There's a pasta bar. What about that?'

When they are perched at the small round table, have ordered and are sipping their first glass of wine Helge takes an envelope from her shoulder bag and passes it across the table.

'Here is another letter for you. I think it is from the same writer.'

Hetty opens out the now familiar photocopy which begins like the last one: *Pater carissime mi* ...

'It is right do you think?'

'I'm sure it is. I'm very grateful.'

In return she offers Helge her translation. 'I brought this along in case you'd like to read it. But maybe you didn't need to. Maybe your Latin is better than mine ... '

'Not at all. I haven't studied it. I should like very much to know what it is you are pursuing.'

Hetty thinks suddenly that she would like to know too, and that if Helge asks her why she's so interested she won't be able to answer. Instead she says, 'Tell me something about yourself. There wasn't time to ask you at the conference.' She's aware of the clumsiness of her question.

'I am at the University of Saarbrucken, a very junior lecturer. I try to alter, no I mean adjust I think, the balance of history a little in favour of women with the study of social change. I have an apartment in the city.'

'You live alone?'

'Yes, now I do.' The question and its answer hang between them like smoke from a shared cigarette, that discredited erotic symbol from a thousand movies.

'When are you going back?'

'In two days' time. And you?'

'Oh I'm quite flexible. I'm staying with a friend I haven't seen for a long time. I don't think she'll turn me out.'

'So perhaps we could meet again tomorrow?'

'Yes, yes we could.'

'Perhaps there is a concert or the theatre you have not seen?'

'I haven't seen anything. I live a very quiet life in the sticks ... the country.'

'In the sticks. The country? I like that. Sticks are pieces of wood yes?'

'Twigs, small branches or wood for lighting a fire, kindling. I think it was probably an Americanism or Australian. Anyway that's where I live.'

'With your English garden.'

'Yes my garden.' It seems very far away, Alice's glimpsed landscape through the little door she had to kneel down to put her eye to.

'Do you like to go to a concert or the theatre?'

'A concert would be best. Plays can be an unknown quantity.'

'And for me the language is not so easy.'

'I'll buy a paper and see what's on.'

'Shall I telephone you at your friend's house?'

'Yes, yes do.'

Hetty watches Helge at her spaghetti, the spatulate fingers with straight, cut clean nails deftly twirling the strings into her mouth, and hopes she is eating as tidily, that her lipstick isn't smeared, that there's no sauce on her chin.

'This afternoon I must go to the Museum of Labour and meet a Mr Mackilroy. We are hoping to exchange exhibitions with them. You know this museum?'

'I've heard of it but I've never been there. What time is your meeting?'

'Two-thirty.'

'Then you must go soon. I think it's somewhere in the East End of London, the old docks perhaps.'

Helge takes a typed letter from her bag. 'Limehouse Town Hall. Is that far?'

'Yes it is. I'll get the bill. This is on me.' Quite as if she's used to it Hetty signals the waitress.

'I can't permit you to pay.'

'Why not! You're a guest.'

'They say in the letter I should take the Docklands Light Railway from Tower Hill.'

'I expect that's right. I've got a tube map in the back of my diary. We'll look up how you get to Tower Hill.'

Hetty gets out her diary and traces the route. 'Can you see?' She puts out her finger. Helge leans across. Hetty turns the map around to face her and Helge puts out her hand. For a moment they touch and then look straight at each other, the contact Hetty has managed to avoid up till now, knowing instinctively though without making it consciously precise in her mind what it might mean, what white water she might be embarking on.

'Time was away and somewhere else . . . ' she remembers, conscious of Helge's face and their touched hands and of all the world outside holding its breath. 'Do you see,' she manages to ask, 'Tottenham Court Road on the Central Line, the red one to Liverpool Street and then the yellow Circle Line to Tower Hill.' She might have been offering a magic formula instead of directions for Limehouse.

'It's a very old part of London. It used to be the Chinese quarter where the sailors went for girls.'

'But not now?'

'Now it's gentrified and politicians and television directors live there. But the local council is still socialist, I think. But you must go. It will take you a long time.'

They are out on the street again. 'Until tomorrow. I will telephone.' Helge bends her head forward and quickly kisses Hetty's cheek with a soft pressure of her lips and then is gone, walking briskly up Great Russell Street while Hetty turns away, her heart thudding so painfully she's seriously afraid she might be sick or that her trembling legs won't carry her.

As it is she only makes it to Russell Square where she sinks on to a bench not already populated. She wishes she hadn't given up smoking. She wishes she had a drink, anything that would calm this crazy flux of adrenalin. She knows now she's on the edge of that abyss of being in love if indeed she hasn't toppled down and down already. A song comes back to her from the old Jack days, admonishing, mocking.

'I'm not in love so don't forget it,
It's just a silly phase I'm going through.
I'm not in love no no . . . '

Even the three fountains in the middle are stilled as if struck by a witch's hand. On the next bench a boy and girl are talking, touching each other with the intimacy of those whose bodies know the smell and feel and shape of the other and for whom the knowledge hasn't grown stale to that point where the self reasserts its sovereignty. Hetty looks at her watch, calmer now, able to go on, wondering how long she's sat there.

A boy is crouched in the underground tunnel beyond the lift, a piece of cardboard round his neck on a string like a child's bib that reads: 'Homeless and Hungary'. Perhaps it's the same boy from the bench in the square she had seen all those aeons before. She puts a pound coin in his battered trilby hat sitting on the floor beside him. His head is bent and he doesn't look up as her small round of fool's gold plops softly down. He has the turnip pallor of the imprisoned. Hetty would like to pull him up and take him away to fresh air and good food and hot baths but she knows that such an individual act of charity is both pointless and patronising. She remembers the *scunizzi* of Naples, the first time she went there on that student jaunt in the late 1950s, the shock of their spindly persistence, the dirty, clutching, monkey hands, and once, when their group had stopped to rest on a stone seat under the feathered palms overlooking the blue bay, a woman in a tired, rusty black dress cradling a baby as hollowed out as herself stretching out a hand that seemed to be joined only a length of bone. It was impossible to tell whether she was a professional and the sight of a few coins would bring a whole tribe out of the surrounding alleys or whether she was indeed Our Lady of the Destitute in search of an epiphany for her rickety child.

There's no answer to Hetty's ring at the door when she reaches the house so she lets herself in with the key Sandy's given her, grateful to be alone and goes upstairs to her room where she drops off her jacket and shoes, undoes the waistband of her skirt and lies down on the bed to fall asleep at once. She dreams she's Europa being carried away by a small black bull that grows smaller under her as she seems to swell but still rushes onwards with a fierce energy she can't control.

Sandy is knocking on the door and calling: 'Hetty, I've made some tea.'

Hetty wakes confused. 'Thanks, I'll come down.' She goes into the bathroom and fills her cupped hands with cold water to bury her face in and then goes downstairs to the kitchen.

'The evenings are starting to draw in,' Sandy says. 'I hate it, don't you?'

'Have you got a paper I could look at? I'm supposed to find a concert we might go to.'

'Try the *Guardian*, behind the bread bin. How was your day? Where did you go?'

'The British Museum. I hadn't been there for years. It was full of people.'

'It always is these days. All the world is on the move, inspecting each other's cultural washing: all those combs and hair pins, and buttons and bits of broken china, and deities of course. All over the world rooms full of variations on the same theme, the accoutrements of living. My new job makes me cynical. Sometimes, I can only see history as a series of backdrops put together so the soap opera can go in front of them.'

'That's one way of looking at it, and probably just as valid as any other.'

'Do you think Bill has affairs in some or all of these countries he's always going to?'

'Do you think he does?'

'I always told myself he hadn't got time but sometimes lately I've wondered. I expect he wonders about me too, left behind. I hope he does. Have you found anything?'

'There's Monteverdi. It seems more neutral than Beethoven or Elgar. St John's Smith Square. Where's that?'

'Just off the Embankment, near the Houses of Parliament. She might not like it.'

'What? Monteverdi?'

'Countertenors neighing in Latin. Not everyone's cup of tea. Oh, take no notice of me. I'm jealous; no not jealous, envious.'

'Envious?'

'Because you're starting something new. You are, aren't you?'

'What do you mean?'

'Come off it Hetty, I can see. Have you done it before?'

'What? Done what?'

'Had an affair with a woman. I've sometimes thought I might. It wouldn't be such a betrayal of Bill. But then that's nonsense. People are people. You're very much in the fashion. There's a lot of it about, especially in the media world.'

Hetty is shocked, unable to answer as Sandy goes on. She hadn't thought in those terms, hadn't thought at all. She had just gone along, responded. Suddenly she's required to embed fragile things in concrete or amber, engrave them on crystal so that they're set fast and can be observed, appraised by others.

'I've never thought of it. I don't know that I'm thinking of it now.'

'Why haven't you thought of it? Didn't you think about us? At Queen's I mean.'

'Did you?'

'In a way. That is I thought about what other people would think when they always saw us together.'

'But there were the boys, Derek and Evan. We were a foursome.'

'No we weren't. I never fancied Evan. Nothing happened between us. I know you went to bed with Derek but that was just trying it on for size if you'll forgive me. You weren't in love with him. You and I were closer.'

Hetty can't deny this, partly because to do so would seem rude and possibly give pain, and partly because it's largely true. Instead she says: 'I don't think I knew such things were possible then. Did you?'

'Yes, yes I did. You see I'd had a friend at school and was in love with. We never did anything physical about it.'

'Oh, I had crushes at school.'

'This wasn't a crush. It was real.'

'I think I thought that it was just a phase you went through at all-girls' schools, you know: falling for prefects and favourite teachers, until you met boys and then that was the real thing. I was very ignorant. I had to learn about sex in biology lessons and from *Lady Chatterley's Lover* and those talks you and I used to have. My parents behaved as though sex didn't exist. Maybe that's why they didn't have any children of their own. As for homosexuality ...' Hetty brings out the word, tonguing its syllables deliberately, facing it.

'Sodom and Gomorrah! They were religious weren't they?'

'Chapel. I've never told you, I've never told anyone; when the legislation went through that said adopted children had the right to know who their natural parents were after they came of age, I wrote to the society I was adopted from and asked them if they had any record of my real parents. I didn't want to do anything about it, didn't want to trace them, I just wanted to know, like settling a historical fact. They told me my mother was a bus conductress in Southampton and my father was a Free French sailor. So technically I'm half-French. I never told my adopted mother I'd found out. It didn't seem kind.'

Hetty remembers the fortnightly visits to the old people's home where the mother who'd brought her up had wandered in and out of lucidity as through a maze that sometimes opened into a half circle with a seat where she could rest and sometimes lowered its hedge to show a distant prospect, clear and open which she could glimpse but never reach, before enclosing her with its dark narrow lanes again.

'Anyway technically I'm half-French and maybe if I'd known that from the beginning it would have made some sort of difference.'

'How do you mean?'

'Well, it's somehow liberating, less conformist.'

'Knowledge is power. That sort of stuff?'

'That's it.'

'We've strayed from the main point,' Sandy is saying firmly when the telephone begins to call and she puts down her teacup and goes out of the room. Hetty stands listening to the silence when the receiver is picked up and is ready, heart pounding again, when Sandy comes back saying with a smile and raised eyebrows: 'For you.'

Helge's voice is very collected. If her heart is thudding it doesn't make her speech shaky. 'Hello. Have you found something that we might visit?'

'How do you like Monteverdi?'

'Oh very much indeed. There is a performance?'

'Tomorrow, yes. In a church.'

'How interesting. Where shall we meet?'

'Outside the west door of Westminster Abbey? The main entrance. That should be easy.'

'At what o'clock?'

'Seven? The concert begins at seven-thirty. Unless you'd like a drink beforehand?'

'That would be good.'

'Okay then. Six-thirty at the Abbey. How was your day? Did you get to the meeting in time?'

'I was a little late but it didn't matter. I have to go again tomorrow and then all will be settled. Have you translated the letter yet?'

Hetty laughs. 'Good god no! I need a dictionary and several days' hard work.' She realises she must end the conversation and go back to Sandy but she doesn't know how, and in any case she isn't eager to meet Sandy's penetrating examination and knowing smile. She's let off the hook by the sound of the pips, followed by a falling coin.

'I have only ten pence. I must say goodbye. Until tomorrow at six-thirty at the Westminster Abbey. Sleep well.'

'And you.' Renewed pips cut her off. Hetty puts down the receiver. When she gets back to the kitchen Sandy has replaced their dirty cups with glasses of whisky.

'I thought you'd need a pick-me-up.' She lifts her glass. 'Here's looking at you kid,' she too toasts Hetty in the words they always used. 'And here's to your French *papa.* I think you're going to need his patronage.'

'I don't know,' Hetty says uneasily. 'Probably nothing will happen.'

They change the subject then and talk of other times and people, easy with each other now, an old unmarried couple and this night Hetty sleeps soundly and wakes in the morning able to tell herself she's been 'imagining things' which was her mother's formula for dealing with the potentially untoward.

# Christopher Barnes

## The Lurex Years

September's hyperphysic mushrooms
withering to nibbles
like fodder-grass roots, dried out
to chomp in rainmaking June.
It's Moortime, cheap-jacks, crystal gazer's caravans,
whirlblast capsules
and a funfair full
of good-time chickabiddy hunks.

My eyes swerve along the chrome and denim,
the trundling bowl of the waltzer,
even sides dwindling to wires,
the toss of cranky lust
in a steam of clangour-wheels
and 'Groovin' With Mr. Blow'*
knocked out of shifting skins from the amp.

*by Mr. Bloe reissued on Lightening records 1970/78

## The Legislator's View

'We've gone too damned far on sex already.
I don't regard any sex as pleasant, it's
pretty undignified.'
– George Brown MP, on legalising male
   homosexuality (sexual offences bill '67)

...so let us pressure-cook sweetmeat,
wake amoebas of honey into mint tea,
design the true look of an unreal sky,
mitigate the colorants of our hairdressing daily
so that the thumb-twiddling stops.

Suppose we hover our naked ape minds on Zen,
tolerate fluorescence to warm our logics.
Bless us for sitting at ease to music
with off-the-peg humdrum suits to wear
taking the edge off our bodies.

When a wished for sensation jumps up
we shall freeze it with raw water,
recall what it is to be British
and bait any propulsion of life
'till the traumas claw our very hearts.

*Wasafiri Vol. 22, No. 1 March 2007, p. 31*
ISSN 0269-0055 print/ISSN 1747-1508 online © 2007 Wasafiri
http://www.tandf.co.uk/journals      DOI: 10.1080/02690050601097591

# Hide and Seek with Rebels

## TRACING CONTEMPORARY QUEER ART IN CRACKS AND RIPS

Caroline Smith

*I was Cathy's teaching assistant for a photography class at UCLA. The class started at 8am. On the first day I arrived, bleary-eyed and with coffee, Cathy, who was sitting alone in the classroom, ripped open her shirt and said: 'Look what I did!' The word 'pervert' was freshly carved into her chest. Thus began my tutelage with Catherine Opie.[1]*

Los Angeles-based artist Amy Adler's first encounter with the photographer Catherine Opie is a key incident in the understanding of contemporary notions of queerness. The identity of the outsider is graphically visualised here and scratched into Opie's chest in a wilful and transgressive act of marking the body. The etching of the word 'pervert' onto the body of the othered subject provokes a dialogue with heterosexist norms that label difference as deviant and sensational. Opie's dramatic self-exposure, revealing and revelling in cut flesh, invites voyeurism symbolising the slippage between the private arena and the public staging and assertion of difference.

The term 'queer' was reclaimed from its derogatory meaning at the beginning of the 1990s when definitions of gay and lesbian were seen as restrictive. The deconstruction of gender undertaken in works such as Judith Butler's *Gender Trouble* and Eve Kokofsky Sedgwick's *Epistemology of the Closet* demonstrated a crisis in the reliance on essentialist identities and opened up more embracing and inclusive approaches to sexuality. Queer artists have long explored the dissolution of gender boundaries to celebrate multiple positions unanchored to any preconceived notion of hetero-normativity. Unabashedly, queer work confronts the dominant gaze, and yet artistic production cannot be detached from the broader mechanisms of the distribution, critique and consumption of contemporary art. This dialogue between the private and the public, from both within and outside of the margins, is always a tenuous one. This is not only because of

the way in which queer art is framed – at the edges of the art world, or as artist Michael Petry states, its subjection to a 'cleansing through a heterosexual filter' – but also because of counter discourses within the work that cannot be assimilated into the mainstream. The art historian Emmanuel Cooper writes:

> Intrinsic to queer culture is that it is fleeting and unpredictable, it cannot be encouraged or promoted in any regular or routine way, but must exist in the cracks and rips. (26)

Evidence for this 'cleansing heterosexual filter' is demonstrated in the work of many artists, not least Ron Athey whose show *Four Scenes in a Harsh Life*, performed at Minneapolis's Walker Arts Centre in 1994, became a target for the far Right. Though he had never received funding from the National Endowment for the Arts, his name was brought into the public debate on state sponsorship of the arts, leading – albeit indirectly – to cuts in the NEA's budget the following year. The press falsely reported that Athey forced the audience to handle clothes impregnated with his HIV-infected blood and locked the doors of the auditorium. Footage, however, showed the artist and his collaborators passing out blocks coated with his blood to willing audience members. This media hysteria led to the negative perception of Athey's work, and the artist was consequently unable to perform at publicly funded venues throughout the US, Latin America and Europe for nearly a decade. His first show at a public institution in the US after this extended period of exile was in 2005 at LA's Redcat Theatre, which Athey dryly states 'is the experimental backside to Disney's concert hall'. Athey's status as near invisible outlaw has been created from a right-wing agenda (art policy makers and the media) that peddles zero tolerance of transgressive identities and practices. 'The issue [scandal] became bigger than me or my work,' he says. His one-off show at the Hayward Gallery in July 2006 (as part of its major *Undercover Surrealism* exhibition) is arguably then something of a breakthrough. He performed his important work *Solar Anus*, in which he endures

*Wasafiri Vol. 22, No. 1 March 2007, pp. 32–42*

ISSN 0269-0055 print/ISSN 1747-1508 online © 2007 Wasafiri
http://www.tandf.co.uk/journals    DOI: 10.1080/02690050601097609

*Michael Petry,* The Milky Way, and Other Fairy Tales *(2004). Suspended pairs of white glass orbs, dimensions variable. Collection of the Museum of Fine Arts, Houston.*

a series of sadomasochistic and sexual acts. It is a gloriously subversive and baroque interpretation of George Bataille's eponymous essay, which draws equivalences between language, eroticism, cosmology and crime. Athey uses his body 'as an offering or a fetish symbol. The performance is a catharsis'. At the beginning, he stumbles naked into the crowd, negotiating the sea of people by grasping shoulders to reach the stage, his altar. The crowd is complicit, silent witness to a spectacle of masculine deviancy and sublime fragility in which Athey, as the tattooed and pierced outcast (often symbolised within queer iconography by religious martyrs such as the arrow-pierced image of Saint Sebastian), is seen as simultaneously fractured and doubled by performing both live and mediated via a large-scale video projection. Athey notes:

> When I started making theatrical-based performance work, I needed ten to twenty people on stage and multiple video screens. I still think multimedia can be

very effective but I've been challenging myself to strip it down to a one-image durational piece: horrific, yet static.

Athey's performances draw viscerally from his life — notably his formative years. He was raised by Pentecostal fanatics in the suburbs of LA in the 1960s, spoke in tongues from the age of nine and was believed to be a latter-day Jesus Christ by the Pentecostal community. He ran away from home as a teenager and subsequently became a heroin addict. He then turned his experience of religion, his HIV-positive status and his sexuality into a performative critique and exploration of his own history. Emerging from the gay fetish club scene, he first performed in the 1980s with his then boyfriend, Rozz Williams. The intensely homophobic climate caused by the impact of HIV became material for his work:

My work directly responded to the amount of death from HIV around me, my own status and the idea of homos cleaning up their act so they wouldn't be separated from the innocent victims. Along with the blood display, live sex show aspects defiantly became present in my work.

## Making History with Stories and Fairy Tales

Athey deploys uncompromising strategies of self-exposure to comment on society's relationship to homosexuality, blood and corporeal pain. This lived experience causes moral panic amongst the more mainstream and conservative elements of the media, the political right and the Christian moral majority. Historically the link between an artist's sexuality and her/his artwork has been clouded by a dominant discourse or erased altogether. In June this year, the National Portrait Gallery held a public discussion titled *Queering the Portrait* that set out to assess and understand interpretations of queerness through its own collection. While the seminar was only a few hours long (and initiated by an external agency: the Pride Legacy Project), it showed that a major public institution was finally open to raiding its own archive in order to assess queerness. One of the speakers, Emmanuel Cooper, made the necessity of storytelling traditions that pass from generation to generation clear. He pointed out that in the absence of an artist's official biography, deeper meanings within the artwork are often unseen. Queer history is not written into the heterosexual canon and consequently it is left open to whimsical interpretation, whispers and hearsay.

Michael Petry, born in El Paso and now based in London, used this oral transmission of queer history to construct *Hidden Histories*, a major document (also an exhibition) of twentieth-century male same-sex lovers. The biographies of Robert Mapplethorpe, Robert Rauschenberg and Felix Gonzales-Torres along with one hundred other men are reassessed to show same-sex lovers working within oppressive political and social climates. He writes:

*Michael Petry,* BB58 *(2006). Glass, EPNS silver object.*

*Michael Petry,* In the Garden of Eden *(2006). Detail view of yew wood.*

A horizontal reading of history as a heterosexual filter must be lifted from prevailing interpretations of the work of same-sex lovers. The exhibition looks at various aspects of these findings by placing examples of works from an unacknowledged queer gaze, and in so doing allows gay/straight audiences the chance to see these works anew.

Shown at The New Art Gallery in Walsall in 2004, Petry's project can be seen as a wider social exploration in which to contextualise his own work. In contrast to the literal and lived arena presented by Athey, Petry transforms materials and their cultural value into sensual installations and sculpture that celebrate male sexuality and desire. Homosexuality is deliberately veiled, implied by the works' titles and woven into the work with codified signifiers and reoccurring motifs. Desire and sexuality are played out through a ghosting of the male gay body as Petry often uses the dimensions of his own body within his installations. This sets up a dynamic interplay between corporeal absence and presence.

References within Petry's work, which include high-value cultural objects such as leather, fresh-water pearls, whole cowhides and solid gold wire as well as the throwaway and déclassé, explore what it is to be a gay man. *The Milky Way and Other Fairy Tales* (2004) was an epic installation in which fifty-one pairs of hand-blown orbs were suspended within the Sundaram Tagore Gallery in New York. Together with pearls sewn into colourfully dyed cowhides on the walls, the work at first glance seemed to present a cosmic constellation where

*Michael Petry,* The Treasure of Memory *(2001/6). Blown glass, rope, metal. Collection of the Museum of Arts and Design, New York.*

lands are mapped out with jewels, a representation of an ethereal cosmos. However, the pearls on cowhide represent the trajectories of actual ejaculations, traced from 'money shots' in gay porn films and the colour on the cowhides represents the 'hanky code', in which gay men wear different colour hankies in their back pockets as a cruising device to show which sex game fetish is preferred. When a young woman wears a pearl necklace in historical Western paintings it denotes her virginal status. By appropriating this signifier of a perceived purity, Petry subverts historical notions of heterosexual beauty and eroticism into contemporary tropes of homoerotic desire. He 'writes' his own body into the work by the placement of the suspended glass balls — at the centre of the constellation is a ball hung at the height of his testicles. He presents a tapestry of glory holes, porno videos and ejaculate to explore a conflation of public and private desire.[2] *Tie a Knot in It* comprises a variety of balls made by the artist's repeated knotting of materials such as gold, black leather or green twine. A variety of ropes drilled into the wall at neck height enabled the viewer to interact and play, thus the complicity and interaction of the viewer were encouraged. Petry explains:

Each knot represents an ejaculate and represents fulfilment. There's a scary feeling to touching the rope because of the historical implications of hangings and there's also the erotic associations with auto-erotic asphyxiation. I'm using different types of rope — from garden material to paratrooper cord. I like the idea of getting involved with something without knowing.

Similarly, in *The Lovers*, in which Petry combines electroplated nickel silver bowls with solidified molten glass, both mainstream cultural references relating to a kitsch, bourgeois England and the act of bare-backing ('the act of unsafe sex in which a hot fluid passes through into an unsafe receptacle') are combined. The results are a series of heavy, bulbous phalluses with gaping sexualised orifices and amorphously fused body parts masquerading as decorative craft-based sculpture. Petry's comments on gay masculinity include a performance with *Web Portraits* in which he asked men from gay chat sites to send pictures of their ejaculations.

They are records of performances. Because it's from the web, you don't know if it's from that man, even if it is from a gay man. You don't know if it's real, but the work is about how people wish to be depicted.

Amy Adler, Once In Love With Amy *(1997). Five Cibachrome prints, 22 ×30 inches each (detail). Courtesy Acme, Los Angeles.*

Petry explores desire and pleasure by symbolising the act of both private practice between gay men and the public consumption of porn movies. He states: 'I don't make work about me having sex. I'm not interested in being a voyeur.' However, he recounts a humorous anecdote of an older female viewer who once asked him why the work was titled *London Cops* when she was looking at the pearls on dyed blue leather. Petry is clear that it is not his role to articulate the queer references in the work. 'There's written documentation of that,' he states. 'If someone wants to know, they don't have to look far.' This statement is evidence of Petry's ability to play with multiple cultural meanings. In other words, the queer component can remain knowingly hidden and it is this act of remaining both hidden and visible that is key. Where the work is shown and to whom it is shown is significant as it causes interference with the dominant gaze. US editor Amy Scholder writes:

> Whilst essentially sharing an outsider position queer artworks are nonetheless contingent, however marginally, upon the signs and narratives of dominant culture. They are about being marginalised for a sexuality that deviates from the norm, yet engaging with the world, reading cultural works with a subversive gaze. This position is informed by the

knowledge of sex as power, and is aware of the subversive possibilities of that power. (178)

## In Pursuit of Fictional Selves

The genre of photography has traditionally provided rich potential for the subversion of this power. The still image's indexical relationship to reality, together with its alignment as a document fixed in time and place, have enabled artists such as Wolfgang Tillmans to show a young generation previously absent from UK media representation. Catherine Opie made visible the LA leather dyke community when she photographed the series *Being and Having* in 1991. Amy Adler, who was under the tutelage of Opie, has worked with portraits taken of her as a child and in her late teens when she had been seen as a model and object of desire. Adler subverts patriarchal power by fabricating the work in different media and, at each evolutionary turn, destroying the older work and laying the past to rest. The resultant images nod to the blurring of media in the work of Chuck Close, and the replication of historical artworks by Sherrie Levine (Duchamp's *Fountain*) — both of whom have influenced Adler. Her series 'Once in Love with Amy' (1997) takes portraits made of her by an older woman when she was nineteen. She states that:

Amy Adler. *Amy Adler Photographs Leonardo DiCaprio (2001). Six Cibachrome prints, 48 ×60 inches each (detail), 2001. Courtesy Acme, Los Angeles.*

*Kelli Connell,* Interrupted *(2002). Digital Lambda Photograph, 30 × 30 inches.*

Using photos taken of me when I was nineteen was important because it implied that I had chosen to be there, and that I was looking back at her, not just being looked at by her. This, I believe, causes the position of the viewer to 'slip' from the assumption that it is a male gazing at a younger woman's body. Possibly, this 'slipping' is 'queer' in the sense that it shifts from an established, 'heteronormative' position. Sometimes the desire enacted in my work is in fact, 'heteronormative'. I want to be able to work with that option available as well.

In her series, 'Amy Adler Photographs Leonardo Di Caprio' (2001), desire is played out by the tactic of subversion. In these photos the actor, Hollywood's poster boy of youthful androgyny, is drawn as a seemingly ordinary boy from the street. Pale, dishevelled and coy-looking, his eyes never confront the viewer, leaving intact an imagined private and intimate relationship between him and Adler, aided and abetted by Adler's act of writing herself into the title of the series. She explains:

I picked him for the seeming impossibility of my having a moment alone with him. I kept secretly hoping he wouldn't show up at the various openings I had with the work because I felt the intimacy needed to remain between us and us alone for the piece to really exist.

Adler's portraits, whether she is in them or not, engage with the notion of herself as an elusive character who simultaneously occupies the role of model, photographer, director and painter. For the viewer, chasing an image of Amy through the various media she uses means imagining a series of fictions that interact with our expectations of the portrait and of photography. She offers up the possibility of playing other ages and genders, creating an archive of identities, ones that read as 'queer', as the positions remain unfixed, unanchored and unresolved.

Mutating identities are also explored in the work of Texas-born photographer Kelli Connell. Her series titled *Double Life*, started in 2001, is an ongoing enquiry into notions of the self and gender in photographic portraiture. The series charts the lives of two lesbian lovers who re-enact scenes from a modern-day relationship: make love, go out and get drunk, go on holiday, drink early morning coffee, hang out the washing and

*Kelli Connell,* Window Shopping *(2005). Digital Lambda Photograph, 25 × 40 inches.*

try for a baby. However, whereas Adler's work is played out between the cracks of various media and various selves, Connell's work comprises 'realistic' moments from a fictional autobiography. Her model (played by photographer and friend, Kiba Jakobson), takes on the role of both lovers. Connell creates these realistic but impossible scenes through the use of Photoshop. Jakobson is not a representation of another subject, but

> she becomes my 'self' and an 'other', just as the roles that she plays are at once the same person and two different characters in a relationship. One of the main reasons I decided to use a model was to be able to have control over this, especially as I needed to make sure that eye contact and physical touching would need to look believable between the two 'selves'. Doing this by using me would be very difficult. People still believe that these are self portraits – even when I am standing right next to the image. Even the model sees less of her inner personality and more of mine in the work.

Connell's work draws on the performance of private behaviours and public signifiers that are the composite elements of the family photo album. Documenting rites of passage and the marking of age through dress, uniform and hair are fundamental to a family's memory bank. However, by appropriating conventions from fashion photography and blurring the staged *mise en scène* with the aesthetics of the snapshot, the real with the mirrored

double, Connell subverts the comforting domestic role played out by the family album. She shows instead the performance of gender and the photo as constructs, where the double disrupts a reading of the images as signifying a 'real', lived relationship. Queer artist and curator Nayland Blake writes of queer artists needing to reconstruct the institution of family in order to show a different lived experience:

> Queer people are the only minority whose culture is not transmitted within the family. Indeed, the assertion of one's queer identity is often made as a form of contradiction to familial identity. Thus for queer people all of the words that serve as touchstones for cultural identification – family, home, people, neighbourhood, heritage – must be recognised as constructions for and by the individual members of that community. (12)

*Interrupted* (2002) shows the arm and torso of what is assumed to be a man (identified only by the masculine shirt). It is the only appearance made by a third character in the series and suggests a sudden, disquieting intrusion. The image can be read in many ways. Though the ominous character is actually Jakobson, the image reminds the viewer that this queer world created by Connell is sharply different to and at odds with a perceived mainstream hetero-normative one. On another level, Connell is drawing on notions of a

*Kelli Connell*, Pregnancy Test *(2004). Digital Lambda Photograph, 30 × 40 inches.*

female masculinity in which maleness – seen through the character's shirt and posture – is independent of gender and can be performed at will.[3] Connell states:

> The model is very 'feminine' in real life. I have always been fascinated by the ambiguity of androgynous males and females. I am interested in the spaces in between the definitions – straight, gay, bisexual – and how these spaces are always moving. A couple of males came up to me after a lecture and thanked me for being so honest. They said that they could identify with the 'selves' in the work. They felt that a lot of pressure was put on how males should be in society and that even though the characters in my work are female, this work made them ask questions.

Connell draws references from queer art history to which she was exposed at art school in the late 1990s. Catherine Opie and Claude Cahun have both influenced her. Adler also stresses that nowadays there is more queer representation:

> My own views were shaped in the 1970s and 1980s where characters like Jodie Foster, River Phoenix and Mariel Hemingway held a lot of charge for their ambiguous sexuality. I grew up making projections – for example imagining that film *The Blue Lagoon* represented first love. To me that meant with a girl I was in love with. I learnt to make my own story stretch around the heteronormative one. Today I don't think kids have to make the same kind of enormous leap as I did.

## Trouble in the Ghetto

Increasing the exposure of queer work is not only reliant on it being written into mainstream art history. What is also important is how the notion of 'queer' itself is shifting. In the mid-1990s an exhibition at Berkeley's University Art Museum in the US was a landmark in its promotion of queer aesthetics. Curated by Nayland Blake, 'In A Different Light: Visual Culture, Sexual Identity, Queer Practice' sidestepped artists' biographies, choosing instead to survey works from straight and queer artists over the last thirty years. It aimed to explore the resonance created by queerness independent of sexuality. Sexual orientation was unspecified so that the meanings of objects and artworks could float free to enable a fresh dialogue between the past and present. Blake asserts that gay and lesbian aesthetic styles intersect with mainstream art

*Nicole Eisenman,* Alice in Wonderland *(1996). Ink on paper,
30 × 22½ inches.*

practice in complex ways and are not constrained to an artist's
sexual identity:

> If identifiable gay or lesbian aesthetic styles or
> sensibilities exist, they exist in multiplicity, and in
> complex intersection with mainstream art practice.
> They are emanations of complex, fluid sociological
> constructs, never simply gay or lesbian. (6)

In this broad cross-generational context, the impact of
visual arts, together with the intersection of genres and
relationships between writers and artists was explored. Works
were organised thematically under pithy titles such as 'Self'
and 'Drag'. It was a seductive tactic in which queer history
(notably the identity politics of the 1980s, the political and
social climate in which gay and lesbian work was made) is
seen to be dislocated from and imagined anew through the
perspective of the present. Shifting the question from how gay
and lesbian artists are making work to how queer artists look
at the world serves as a universalising strategy and is inclusive
of a wider art-making community that identifies with
queerness. In this light, Turner prizewinner Grayson Perry's
work could be situated within this new paradigm. His
engagement with transvestitism, his subversion of the
domestic and traditionally female craft-based practice
of making ceramics, together with his curiosity about

transgressive practices such as sadomasochism that are
embedded in his recent show, *The Charms of Lincolnshire* at
Victoria Miro (2006), certainly suggests that his work may be
read as queer on one level. Catherine Grant, an art historian
and speaker at *Queering the Portrait*, discussed Sam Taylor
Wood's *Sleep*, a portrait of footballer David Beckham that
evidently pays homage to Andy Warhol's movie *Sleep* (1963).
The work, she argues, can be read 'queerly':

> David Beckham is shown sleeping, shot from the
> perspective of lying in bed next to him. This portrait is
> a tongue-in-cheek acknowledgement of what we might
> want to get out of a picture of him — namely a fantasy
> of being intimate with him. Rather than presenting him
> in a traditional portrait manner, this could be seen as a
> portrait of desire, rather than a portrait of individual
> celebrity. Whose desire is being portrayed is up to the
> viewer.[5]

This is arguably a more inclusive approach that engages
with work seemingly existing neither in one place nor another
in terms of gender and sexual orientation. It is interesting that
some of the artists exhibited in *In A Different Light*; Karen
Walker, Nan Goldin, Catherine Opie and Nicole Eisenman, were
also shown two years earlier in *Bad Girls* at the ICA and at
UCLA. Both exhibitions explored a highly diversified feminist
movement through works that were anti-ideological. *Bad Girls*
was criticised for ghettoising women's work into a slick and
dismissive brand where women regress into mere girls who
play up, act naughty and are dismissed to the back room to
make artwork. Eisenman has resolutely distanced herself from
the label lesbian or even feminist artist. She states:

> I would never think about these terms in 1994. The
> labelling of *Bad Girls* – the tag, the bad girl lesbian
> artist – was external to my way of working. I don't work
> from a political place. It's my personal viewpoint.
> There are artists who set out to deliberately deal with
> identity in their work. I didn't set out with that mission;
> I just stumbled into that ditch by accident.

Eisenman's work – resolutely queer, post-punk and
ferocious – uncompromisingly challenges the canon of male
art history. *Self-portrait with Exploded Whitney*, a vast
neoclassical mural that covered the walls of the Whitney
Biennale in 1995, depicted the Museum bombed, its paintings
scattered as administrators and the press attempt to grab the
remains. Eisenman is seen with her back to the viewer,
painting the only remaining wall. She draws on the vernacular
of the underground comic genre and appropriates freely from
art history.

> I looked at a lot of the old cartoonists when growing
> up, Ernie Bushmiller, George Herriman, Saul Steinberg,
> Chas Adams and Edward Gorey. My parents had all
> that stuff lying around the house. But that stuff wasn't
> underground, it was in the daily newspapers and the
> New Yorker magazine. I got into underground comics in

*Nicole Eisenma,* Self-portrait with Exploding Whitney *(April–June 1995). Wall mural for the Whitney Biennial.*

college — the early 'zines in the 1980s were all about boys and their punk bands, I dug that scene.

Her drawings and paintings depict females as warriors, Amazons and superheroes to subvert the image of the female subject as passive object. *Alice In Wonderland* (1996) shows her version of Lewis Carroll's heroine, where Alice's head disappears up the trademark skimpy hot pants of Wonder Woman. Elsewhere, her family portrait, where members mutilate genitalia, eat excrement and masturbate in front of one another, fractures the white-picket fence profile of the all-American suburban family. In *Cowgirls* (1996) the protagonists urinate and defecate as they take a break from duties, presented within a rococo frame. She creates a chaotic world seen through a lens of urban realism in which everything – including politically correct references to dyke culture – is assimilated into her universe. From pop culture to porn to classical art, irreverent humour is at the core of her practice:

> The humour is not conscious. It has just happened. Comedy is tragedy for funny people and its sources are the same: it's the big bog of pain we all slog around in. I have claimed in the past not to be angry but I don't think I recognised my anger as 'anger'. I think I'm SO angry it's off the charts and doesn't even compute as anger. It computes as humour. Shit seems funny to me. But mostly 'hurty' funny. Once you give any

thought to the politics of an identity, you can't be angry.

Eisenman has recently brought out a fanzine, *Ridykelouse*, published through her gallery, Leo Koenig in New York, an irreverent and hilarious take on contemporary dyke culture. Including work by Kathe Burkhardt, Nicola Tyson and Eisenman herself, it is celebratory and politically incorrect. *Charles Saatchi's Dick*, Christian Lemmerz's image of male genitalia dumped in a toilet, is one example. It is a sharp reaction to the serious, out and proud stance of younger collectives in New York, such as Lesbians to the Rescue (LTTR), formed in 2001, which engage in creating diverse spaces for queer artistic production as a tactic of resistance towards the dominant discourse. The group has a strategy of building queer communities by producing a fanzine and organising performances and screenings (the most recent seen within the *London Gay and Lesbian Film Festival,* 2006). The collective reinvents the mainstream notion of the outlaw by using post-punk strategies and celebrates queer artistic production at the margins.

There are multiple strategies employed by queer artists. Detached from the dominant discourse, their work constructs other pleasures, reconfiguring the body, appropriating archives and genres, imagining biographies and claiming a counter-heritage. Is queer art still in and out of the margins, and in the cracks? Most of the artists featured in this article have gallery representation, enjoy solo shows and their work has been critically evaluated within funded publications. Arguably, their position within the art world extends and perhaps, in some cases, overwrites their queerness. Nicole Eisenman states that there are 'undoubtedly these cracks that have been cemented over by the academy. Gay work is part of the establishment but the "gay" part is left in those cracks.'

Throughout the research for this article, Eisenman's quote has continually rung true. Several artists did not wish to be included and one is left wondering if the term 'queer' is seen as being too loaded, too outdated or just too particular to be attached to artists and works that can obviously be read in a myriad of ways. Not to identify one's work as queer has the lure of attracting wider audiences and greater funding opportunities. LTTR makes a point of stressing that the collective is self-financed and therefore free from the economic values and agendas of investors. Eisenman ironically asserts, 'we are all feminists now', and by extension, if Judith Butler's vision was correct, with the future dissolution of heterosexual categories, perhaps we are all queer, our identities in a constant state of flux.

Certainly queer work that resides in a ghetto is problematic as it can seem to place work in a category into which all marginal identities neatly fit. Work in the ghetto remains largely unseen and stands independent of the mainstream. Yet, however loaded and reductive the perception of the term queer this work needs to be exposed, celebrated and critiqued. The collision of transformative and transitory exchanges between work that is read queerly and normative discourse cannot be overlooked. Public institutions are slowly opening their traditionally conservative doors to what niche events and queer scene hotspots have been doing for years — such as Bar Wotever in the UK that screens queer film and stages performance. At the margins or in the mainstream, there is a provocative dialogue between normative and queer discourse that continues to set the latter apart. Queer work, whether read queerly or created from an artist's biography cannot be commodified. Key to its spirit is reconfiguring lived experience so that we may look anew at cultural history. Those crammed into the Hayward Gallery straining to see Athey's spectacle and viewers of Petry's work who become integral

players are performances that rely on a complicit public rather than the notion of queer culture as fleeting and hard to promote. Those cracks and rips that Cooper identifies are now not so much the static places within which queer art resides and should be celebrated, but the very acts of queerness itself.

## Notes

1   All quotes from artists, unless specified, are from interviews carried out by the author; May–August 2006.
2   A 'glory hole' is a hole made in the wall of a lavatory cubical for the purpose of anonymous sex.
3   Judith Halberstam writes extensively on the essentialism of fixed masculinity in culture that cannot be performed but threatens mainstream discourse, which is conversely accepting and encouraging of a femininity that is performed at will. She explores the acceptance of drag queens in popular culture and the rejection of 'kinging' or drag kings in her book, *Female Masculinity*, Durham and London: Duke University Press (1998).
4   Interview with Grayson Perry for *Attitude* magazine, September 2006. Perry states that he imagined himself in the public situation of winning the Turner Prize — and thinking that the most humiliating act would be to accept the prize in a dress, as Claire, his transvestite self.
5   Art historian Catherine Grant speaking at *Queering the Portrait*, 4 July 2006, at the National Portrait Gallery.

## Works Cited

Blake, Nayland. 'Curating In a Different Light'. *In A Different Light: Visual Culture, Sexual Identity, Queer Practice*. Eds. Nayland Blake, Lawrence Rinder, and Amy Scholder. San Francisco: City Lights Books, 1995. 9–43.
Cooper, Emmanuel. 'Queer Spectacles'. *Outlooks: Lesbian and Gay Sexualities and Visual Cultures*. Eds. Peter Horne and Reina Lewis. London: Routledge, 1996. 13–27.
Petry, Michael. *Hidden Histories: 20th Century: Same Sex Lovers in the Visual Arts*. London: Artmedia Press, 2004.
Scholder, Amy. 'Writing In a Different Light'. *In A Different Light: Visual Culture, Sexual Identity, Queer Practice*. Eds. Nayland Blake, Lawrence Rinder, and Amy Scholder. San Francisco: City Lights Books, 1995. 177–82.

# Miri ya Mikongoe[1]

*Keguro*
*Macharia*

*Gukira Kuri Ngatho*:
Forgive me if I should speak of the impossibility of
  my desire;
*Gukira Kuri Ngatho*:
Forgive me if I should speak of the necessity of my
  desire;
*Gukira Kuri Ngatho*:
And against injunctions.
*No ni hinya muno kuona mugikuyu ugweta na undu*
  *ucio*

[Perhaps one day] people will ask themselves why we
were so bent on ending the rule of silence regarding
what was the noisiest of our preoccupations. In
retrospect, this noise may appear to have been out of
place, but how stronger will seem our persistence in
interpreting it as but the refusal to speak and the order
to remain silent. (Foucault 158)

  Perhaps it is necessary to speak of the truth of desire
  Perhaps it is more important to speak of necessity

Forgive what appear to be my hesitations, my false starts,
my continual shifts, my elisions, my hyperbole, even the
proprietary use of the term 'my'; it is not that I do not want to
proceed, but there are no directions, no rule books, only a
stumbling need to follow the phantasmic roots of the
necessary.
  I struggle to make this discourse familiar, even as I am
held in thrall by its very unfamiliarity. Shall I write, then, of
bodies and pleasures, of acts and conquests, of visions and
vices, tread in the paths of a familiar pornography, a known
terrain . . .
  Perhaps rehearse well-known platitudes, demands for
justice, for freedom, for equality, for rights; believe in the
power of compulsive repetition, incessant pleading, the need
for martyrs or fools . . .
  I start to write of acts and emotions but I am distanced by
the phrases lifted and recycled, used and worn, and I wonder
at their inadequacy, my lack of creativity.

— What is it you write?
— Words.
— What needs to be said is urgent.
— One cannot be careless with form.
  This is not an assertion, nor an affirmation of truth. This is
not an enumeration of something termed oppression or
something experienced as such.
  It *is* a search for something elusive, a necessary fantasy,
the roots of a mythical tree.
  Perhaps the prelude to other stories.

## I: *Gukira*

*Ithaga riene rinogagia ngingo* (Gikuyu proverb)

*Mugathi wa kuona uteaga wa mwene* (Gikuyu proverb)

*Agikuyu moigaga, 'utathiaga eciiragia no nyina urugaga*
*wega'*. Only a contemporary and bastardised cant has it that
what is foreign, learned from foreigners and the process of
travel, is necessarily bad, evil, unworthy. Here I write
specifically to those who would silence me by saying, 'these
are white words, foreign ones'.
  We, the Agikuyu, believe that wisdom is borne in the
blood, that we are a wise people, a people given to discerning
not just the will, but the mysteries of the gods.
   Do I overreach myself?
This shall be a performance, a dance, if you will.


  *Nguina nooyu mwega*
  *Nooyu mwega*
  *Ihai-ihui*


Even the visitors know how to sing. With whom shall you sing?

  *Words from over there, that place, that place over*
  *there, taste like* muhu, *like the ashes that cover dead*
  *bodies. When I say them, my mother covers her ears*
  *and her eyes, my mother beats her breasts and her*
  *thighs: 'you were conceived and reared in pain.'*

  My people (a fiction, a myth, a construction, a necessity).
Stubbornly clannish, we fight for what is ours, for our land, for

*Wasafiri Vol. 22, No. 1 March 2007, pp. 43–49*
ISSN 0269-0055 print/ISSN 1747-1508 online © 2007 Wasafiri
http://www.tandf.co.uk/journals    DOI: 10.1080/02690050601097641

our children, for our ways, for our stories. (And particular fights of language, through language, over language.)

Do not mistake ethnic particularity for ethnic insularity. When I say 'my people' I invoke our myths and histories, our triumphs and failures. When I say 'my people' I kill the myth of the generic African. A product of the imperial imagination, he has never existed. Not African, Gikuyu. When I say 'my people' I invite you to share your stories: tell me of 'your people'.

Perhaps what is difficult is only the beginning. Enacting a particular fight, a struggle over language, over telling and not telling, over hearing and not hearing, over being heard and not being heard. Sometimes I think I am ready to tell and to hear.

At other times, I run away, I hide in the language of visitors, the ones I do not know, the university words, the ones I cannot say, the learned words, the ones with sharp edges spoken by men who speak too fast with sharp tongues like blunt knives that cut, but cut exceedingly slow. (*Ucio ni muturi wa rugano, muturi wa ndeto, mumbi witu.*)

My mother has a son, a son who is called after her father:
She tells him she wishes he had never been born.

## II: Tongues

At each step language marks its own, those to whom shall be revealed the mysteries of the word, the pleasure of play within each letter, each syllable, the indescribable *jouissance*. (It means climax, it means orgasm, a woman's orgasm; does that scare you, that you shall see your mother's nakedness, your sister's nakedness, your brother's wife's nakedness? And do you shake with the fear of it? Or is it your hidden and unnamed desire that so causes your shorts to protrude? Your distended desire?)

I want to write about desire but find myself writing about language. I want to write about love and sex but find myself writing about my mother. At each step, a thwarted desire or a fulfilled one. Does writing dispel ghosts or invite them in?

(The feeling that sometimes my father's ghost hovers over my shoulder, glances approvingly, prods me on, compels me to write beyond myself. Or that he covers his eyes and cries silent tears, silent cold tears. Sometimes I feel those tears falling. Or I imagine them. It is all the same.)

*Menya ati ciugo citiri murio ta tuuhoro, natuo tuuhoro tutiri murio ta turugano.*

I am craving certain stories but find myself stuck at words.
Certain baby steps.

I find myself thrown from one language to another, from one home to another, from one mother to another. And in this movement, this repetition, this redoubling, I wonder if it is possible to write of silence. And of displacement.

Displacement — to identify oneself in a medically derived neologism: homosexual.
Displacement — to write in English from a country that is not my own.
Displacement — to translate an imperfectly remembered language for a foreign audience.

Nothing invokes home like one's mother tongue. (See here a certain myth: there is 'one' tongue above all others, one that bestows identity, bestows a history, a culture, expectations, anticipation; and what of those who have learned to occupy the tongues of displacement? Who have experienced the pleasure of another tongue?)

One does not return to language. One re-encounters language, meets it with one's histories. One woos, seduces, beguiles, entices, and hopes that the pleasure of the encounter lives on in the traces of language that one attempts to capture.

Imperfect orthography is like the touch of a first encounter.[2]

(Shall I write here of the endless curiosity of the Gikuyu child? The way all other children when instructed to do a certain thing follow instructions, but the Gikuyu child asks why a certain thing should be done. This is my uncle's myth, and one of which I am particularly fond.)

It is fascinating to read of my people, the Agikuyu, as agriculturalists, as people who were settled in one area or another, for all our stories invariably involve travel:

*Ugai itha*
*Tene tenu muno ni kwari na anake na airitu, magithii rwimbo...*
*Na ringi*
*Muthuuri egwika uguoi-i, agathii gutura meena athuri aria angi*

*Na ringi*
*Anake makirana magacarie airitu matari thongo*
*Rugano ruteritwo ni ruthiriga?*

I would rather speak of displacement than transition, for transition beckons to and suggests beginnings and endings, origins and destinations, a certain epistemology of travel, or perhaps I simply dislike the metaphysical implications of the word 'transition'.

One learns to embrace the necessity for displacement if not displacement itself.

*Ngwatia Ndai     Ndagwata*
*Ithiaga igicooka*

## III: In Search of a Tongue

Now, there was a time when I felt very bad. I felt very bad because I said, 'Now, if this word does not exist in my language, surely it means that the concept is unheard of.' Unable to find a word in 'my' tongue that referred to 'me', I became very depressed. So, at this time, when I felt very bad, I found myself giving up, putting down my pen, and deciding not to write of certain things, not to try to translate them, accepting the dictates of a language that, seemingly, had rejected me.

So, when I found that there was no word that said what I wanted to say, I decided that the tongue that could not speak of me was not a tongue worth keeping. But, at night, when my mind grew tired, when my resistances no longer functioned, I found myself crooning little songs, falling under the spell of a tongue that I had rejected. And my fights, those many fights over language, assumed massive proportions.

And, more importantly, I began to understand the fiction of language, and the need for myth.

Now, in one of my people's stories, there is a monster, *Irimu*, who often takes the shape of a beautiful man. This monster has two mouths, one where the regular mouth is found on the face, and another at the back of his head, covered by his hair.

I do not know whether this second mouth 'speaks', or serves any function beyond a purely identificatory one, and even that imperfectly. Is there, rather than a tongue that tells the truth of identity, another mouth through which the truth of identity may be found? Fancifully, one may ask whether this idea of a second, concealed mouth pre-shadows modern psychoanalysis. Hidden mouths suggest unspoken histories in which identity floats.

Is there a truth of physiognomy?

I know many men who would like to have a second mouth at the back of their heads so that they could have sex with many other people at the same time instead of making them line up and wait with the painful distensions of unrelieved lust.

In truth, I am more fascinated by the prospects of oral sex with two mouths than I am in deciphering the truth of language or physiognomy.

So what happens to the search for a tongue?

(Certain pathways suggest pleasurable alcoves, multiple interludes, and I am so easily seduced; my problem, I am told, is that I cannot remain focused. But focused to what end? And for what purpose? Pleasure, after all, is my only aim, and the ways of pleasure are surely divorced from the strictures of direction.)

But to continue a certain story: at this point I was feeling pain because I could not find a word to name a concept. And I felt very bad. I felt invisible, unwanted, undesirable.

But surely, I asked, where would a man busy pleasuring two men at the same time, with two different mouths, one in front and one at the back, find time to think of a word to describe himself?

And this seems to me to be a very logical question.

## IV: *Nguina nooyu mwega*

*No o na haria kwi mithemba yacio miingi,*
  *itikoragwo*
*ituitwo mariitwa ma gucikuurana bururi-ini*
  *wa Gikuyu*
(*Gikuyu Grammar Book*)

The all-consuming search for identity within one's language is complicated. I believed, wrongly, that the lack of a word within my language to describe 'me' was a mark of my invisibility, my unworthiness. I concluded that this lack was simultaneously an erasure of people who had been like me, who had shared my desires, who had expressed similar

desires. Yes, I was angry. I had learned that to be excluded, to be erased, to be unacknowledged, was a gesture of violence. Yet these constructions were wildly at odds with how I grew up.

Identity amongst the Agikuyu is always expressed in a relational way. One is the son *of*, the grandson *of*, belongs to the family *of*, comes from the clan *of*. What is most important (and constant) in identity is *of*, the mark of belonging.

*Of* represents a process of inheritance. We inherit our names and their histories. Our names have meanings and histories. My name has a meaning and a history. I like this formulation, for it presents a challenge: whose meaning and whose history? One way of understanding these inherited names and histories is that the old generation lives on in the young, the traits and the characteristics of those who have gone are preserved in their names, and it is the responsibility of those who live to uphold those names and memories.

Again, I ask: whose meaning and whose history?
To conceive of a name as an infinitely played historical loop is boring.

Instead of conceiving merely of a history-bearing name, I want to consider those acquired histories as paradigms, more specifically, to write not of a history-bearing name, but a history-making name.

Do I overreach myself?
'One would think,' Nietzsche writes, 'that history would above all encourage men to be *honest*' (29).

To conceive of history not as a search for truth, but the meeting:mating place of memory, hyperbole, and myth.
– What needs to be said is urgent.
– One cannot be careless with form.
– A theory of responses: tracing over our words.
– Nested in your vocabulary
Rooted in your syntax, I struggle to escape your muting.

One awakens into language
Chafing at imagined restrictions
Or the need for new words
In the absence of singing
Some speak of the prison-house of language

*Rugano ruuru ni rwa gwitungira*
*Ciiko iria iri ho ni cia gwitungira*
*Andu aria mari ruganoini ni a gwitungira*
*Rugano rureekiriro bururi wa gwitungira*
*Muthoomi — Rwikiri bururi uria uukwiyeendera!*

Finding comfort within the regime of disclaimers
Which, in a foreign tongue, or my mother's,
Bear the burden of a strange and unwieldy history
Circumventing the dictates of history
Or the process

*Niingi gutiri ati niri rwekikire*
*Ira; iyo; kiumia kiu kiraathirire?*
*Mwaka ucio uraathirire?*

*Kana miaka ikumi yaathirire?*
*Muthoomi — Ikera mahiinda maria uukwiyendera!*

The children have learned to play
In the neighbour's house
With toys they did not make
And sounds we did not teach them
Shall we fear for their safety?

*Niingi rutiri ati niha rwekikiire*
*Haaha kana haria!*
*Ituura riiri kana riria*
*Rugongo ruuru kana ruuria*
*Muthoomi — Reke rwikikire haria uukwiyendera!*

Have locations lost their power to confine
Or am I still holding your hand, your dress, your
    person?
You keep me here and make me afraid to leave
For in so far as I do not understand you
I fear more the abrasion of a foreign mouth eating my
    afterbirth

*Ningi rutigayaniitie mahinda na nguta*
*Kana na ndagika;*
*Kana na mathaa*
*Kana na mithenya*
*Muthoomi — Gayania mahinda uria ukwiyeendera*

*Ugai litha, nguganire!* (Gikuyu adapted from wa Thiong'o,
*Matigari*, up.)

## V: *Rugano Ruteritwo*

'In the unsayable, useless words lie hidden which we will
claim later'.
(Jabes 49)

*Rugano ruuru ni rwa gwitungira*
*Niingi gutiri ati niri rwekikire*
*Niingi rutiri ati niha rwekikiire*
*Niingi rutigayaniitie mahinda na nguta*

*Tene ni kwari na aanake. Makiendana na irimu. No o matioi ni
irimu. Riu nimainaga o magithii na njira. Aanake aya maari
atano. Umwe wao nionire mwanake aruuga akimenya ati ni
irimu. Irimu rikiruuga ringi na mwanake ungi akiriona na
agicooka na thuutha. Mwanake ungi akiona irimu riaruuga,
akiona riina kanua kangi nake agicooka na thuutha. Aanake
atatu magitigwo.*

A long time ago there were some young men. They fell
in love with an *Irimu*. They did not know he was an
*Irimu*. Now, they were singing as they followed the
*Irimu* back to his house. There were five young men.
One saw the *Irimu* jump and saw he was an *Irimu*. The
*Irimu* jumped again and another young man saw and

turned back. Yet another young man saw *Irimu*'s
second mouth when *Irimu* jumped, and he turned
back. Three young men were left.

*Magithii muno muno mwanake wa gatatu akiona irimu
riaruuga ringi. Ni kwari mitaro irimu riaruugaga. Mwanake uyu
akiona ni irimu. Agicooka. Niarakiitie kuona ati irimu riari na
kanua na haaha igoti. Aanake eeri magitigwo. Aanake acio
makiuga meeguthii nginya makinye kuria mwanake ucio
aikaraga. Magithii, magithii. Kirimu gikaruuga mutaro o
mutaro.*

After a long distance, another young man saw *Irimu*
jump. Kirimu was jumping over ditches. This young
man saw this was an *Irimu*. He turned back. He saw
*Irimu* had a mouth on the back of its head. Two young
men were left. They said they would follow *Irimu* all the
way to its home. They went on, even as *Irimu* kept
jumping over ditches.

*Riakoragwo ri mbeere ya aanake rimatongoirie rikamoonie
mucii. Njuiri ikigayana ringi. Mwanake umwe akiona kanua
igotiini ria Irimu. Agicooka. Mwanake umwe agitigwo.*

*Irimu* was in front of the young men, leading them to
its home. Its hair parted again. One of the young men
saw its second mouth on the back of its head. He
turned back. One young man was left.

*Mwanake uria watigitwo thuutha akiuga ati aguthii nginya
agaakinya kwa mwanake ucio muthaka uguo. Mwanake uyu
ona oona kanua kau kaari igotiini akiuga no eguthii nginya
akoone kwa mwanake ucio!*

This young man who was left said he was going to
follow the beautiful *Irimu* all the way to its house. Even
when he saw the second mouth on the back of *Irimu*'s
head, he insisted on going to *Irimu*'s house!

To find oneself amidst silences one must bend language.
The original rendering of the tale features *airitu*, young
women.[3] But could this not happen with *aanake*, young men?
To survive, one creates counter-stories.

For the Agikuyu, *Irimu*, the monster, is not necessarily
distinguished by any one physical feature, but by action: *Irimu*
eat human flesh. The word *Irimu* bears within it traces of
mental disadvantage – *kirimu* or fool – and improper health —
*murimu* or illness. More importantly, the threat of *Irimu* is not
that it will 'eat' one; the real threat is that *Irimu* will convert
one, will make one lose one's identity through the act of eating
human flesh.

This fear is made abundantly clear in the story *Manga
Manga na Ithe*:

*Muthuuri egwika uguo-i, akagura mutumia. Agura
mutumia-ri, makoima kwao Gikuyu-ini magathii bururi*

*wa marimu. Mathii kuu-ri, magatiga andu ao Gikuyu-*
*ini. Mathii kuu-ri, muthuri-ri, atuikire irimu athii bururi*
*wa marimu. Na mutumia uyu wake-ri, ti irimu. Na*
*mutumia ucio agiikara ota Mugikuyu we ndatuikire*
*kirimu.* (Kabira and Mutahi 124)

A man married a wife. After marrying her, they left the
land of the Agikuyu and went to the land of *Irimu*. They
left all their people in the land of the Agikuyu. When
they went to *Irimu*'s land, the husband became an
*Irimu*. But his wife was not an *Irimu*. His wife lived
like a Mugikuyu and did not become an *Irimu*. (My
trans.)

*Irimu* threatens because it seduces, inducing a desire so
strong that one turns foreign. *Irimu* is a corrupting influence,
an invitation to disavow identity.

## VI: *Miri ya Mikongoe:* Injunctions

*Mundu murume kugwata uria ungi ni mugiro munene*
*utari horohia. Kwiragwo ati mugwato ndangiruuga. No*
*ni hinya muno kuona Mugikuyu ugweta na undu ucio;*
*no tondu wa uria thi itaagaga imaramari, mundu*
*murume angigwata uria ungi nake mugwatwo amenye,*
*matingitigana. Mahuranaga o nginya riria umwe wao*
*ariuragwo.* (Kabetū 105)

Tracking the roots of a mythical tree, abandoning all claims to
a founding story. As elusive as an ethnography of desire.

Hysteria expresses an 'as though', Freud teaches us. It
is the threat of what cannot be named, what is endlessly
played out in the unconscious, a knowing that emerges as
a split, a fissure, an irruption into the social. Hysteria is
failed legislation. Against the injunctions of psychic
censorship, one speaks and forbidden stories emerge. A
community's horror of its hidden stories emerges. Kabetū's
statement records a moment of social hysteria.

We begin with what appears to be a forthright assertion:
'*Mundu murume kugwata uria ungi ni mugiro munene utari*
*horohio*' [Should a man *kugwata* another man, the men
cannot be ritually cleansed].

The root of the term *kugwata* is *gwata*, a word that I shall
insist is impossible to translate:

*Gwata*: take hold of, seize, hold (in the hand) grip;
Adhere, stick to; take on, obtain, acquire;
(in a sexual sense) have intercourse with, rape;
take hold (of) lightly, grope in the dark;
pick and steal
(T G Benson, *Kikuyu-English Dictionary*)

In his acknowledgments, T G Benson outlines, through the
use of proper names, the vexed history of written Gikuyu: Rev.
L J Beecher — Archbishop of East Africa; Mr A R Barlow,
formerly of the Church of Scotland Mission (CMS) in
Kikuyuland; Rev. A W McGregor of the CMS; Rev. Fr Hénéry;
and Rev. Canon Leakey.

To read a history of Gikuyu transcription is to read a history
of scriptural translation. And to follow *gwata* in its biblical
context is to understand, if only partially, the horror and
revulsion with which Kabetū approaches this term.

And the classic biblical injunctions against male
homosexuality do not disappoint us. Genesis 19: 5, the
story of Sodom and Gomorrah, has the men of Sodom
demanding, '*Moimie na gūkū nja tūrī, tūmagwate*' [Bring
them out to us so we might *gwata* them]. In this passage,
we understand *kūgwata* as an act of physical violence, a
violation.

Leviticus 18: 22–23 muddies the waters:

*Ndūkanakome na mūndū mūrume ta ūrīa andū-a-nja*
 *makomagwo nao; nī gūkoruo ūndū ūcio wī thathu;*
*Ningī-rī, ndūkanagwate nyamū ona īrīkū withukie nayo*
. . .

Do not sleep with a man as you do with a woman; such
 an act is impure
Do not *gwata* an animal and defile yourself with it . . .

Verse 22 forbids an analogous act to that performed
with women; not violation, one might say, but the transference
of symbolic and cultural value: 'as with a woman'. Here the
word is '*gukoma*', literally to sleep with, rather than *kūgwata*.
Verse 23 returns us to the horror of violation, linking *kūgwata*
specifically to bestiality. *Kūgwata* is a bestial act, one that
blurs the distinction between man and animal, an act that
defiles.

Perhaps the most interesting biblical verse about
homosexuality, though, is Leviticus 20: 13:

*Na rīrī, mūndū mūrume o na ūrīkū angīgakoma na*
*mūndū mūrume ūrīa ūngī, ta ūrīa mūndū-wa-nja*
*akomagwo nake, andū acio erī nīmekīte ūndū wī thahū,*
*nao matiri hingo matakoragwo; nīo magacokererūo nī*
*thakame yao o ene*

And anytime a male shall *koma* with another male the
way men sleep with women, the two have committed
an impure act, and there is no time that the two shall
not be killed; their own blood shall have turned
against them.

Perhaps this verse authorises Kabetū's writing on
homosexuality, for no other writer on the Agikuyu has so
detailed a text regarding male homosexuality. Among those
who mention it, Kenyatta tells us it did not exist. L S B Leakey,
tells us that it was considered the act of madmen, but he does
not attach a penalty to it, and certainly nothing as severe as
death; John Mbiti tells us that a fine was levied.

Let us continue: Kabetū indicates that this act is a big
taboo ('*mugiro munene*') that cannot be ritually purified ('*utari*
*horohio*'). A limit is introduced, an aporia: the community
cannot cleanse or purify this — what is it? Act? Desire? An
acted-on desire?

An act that cannot be purified. A desire that cannot be understood.

A knowing silence is introduced: '*no ni hinya muno kuona Mugikuyu ugweta na undu ucio*' (But it is very difficult to find a Mugikuyu who will mention such a thing). Enacting his distaste for this 'thing', Kabetū refuses to name it; his readers have presumably understood this 'thing' for what it is; that which cannot be named, that which has no 'proper name', a metonymic slide into the unnamable, the intolerable; this 'thing' – not to be named among Christians – is not to be named among the Agikuyu:

Shall I dare to name this 'thing': anal penetration

I now approach what, for me, is the most interesting part of the text: '*mundu murume angigwata uria ungi nake mugwato amenye, matingitigana*' (if a male *gwata*[s] another male and the *mugwato* [prisoner] discovers, they cannot leave one another).

The statement is laughable, but it is a hysterical laughter.

We laugh at the thought of a male being mounted without his knowledge, at this intricate rape that does not announce itself as such. We laugh, uncomfortably, at an awkward, fumbling expression of desire, an invitation to unread violation as punishable, an enticement to the pleasure of violation. We laugh, sadly, as *kūgwata*, that awkward signifier binds the two men.

'Cannot leave one another' would be a utopic statement if the passage ended there; we could envision two Gikuyu men parting from the tribe to go and live together in the bliss of desire. Sadly, the text does not allow such a reading; rather, we are confronted with a violence that seeks to curtail desire: '*Mahuranaga o nginya riria umwe wao ariuragwo*' [They fight until one of them is killed]. The two men, once joined in desire, are complicitous: there can be no distinction between active and passive, seducer and seduced, *erastes* and *eromenos*. They are both to blame. However, since this is an offence that the community cannot purify, then the two men must fight to the death. Their own blood, as in Leviticus 20: 13, must turn against them.

*Kūgwata*, in Kabetū's text is metaphor and metonymy. It is never innocent, always culpable. It is the accidental grip that is always a violent seizing. It is the inadvertent grasp that is always an act of rape. Strangely, though, *kūgwata* is coded as an act of aggression precisely because it might not be.

Instead, it might be an act of desire, a desired act.

For desire to be mastered a wrongful object of desire must die. One can only speculate about the psychic, social and political consequences for the one left standing.

Sanctioned suicide.

'*No ni hinya muno kuona Mugikuyu ugweta na undu ucio.*'
Homosexual sex.

What, one might ask, is the 'true' object of silence?

I want to know: what is the relationship between silence, pleasure and desire? Is it something like having a 'secret', whose pleasure is ensured only by its always-compromised status: 'I have a secret; I cannot tell you what it is.'

Perhaps silence is not just the absence of speech, but the evacuation of language and, consequently, desire.

A cessation of language is the greatest violence that can be done to the violence of language. (Barthes 159)

A confession. I began this essay in another time frame. Little of the original structure remains. I started writing this essay as a letter to my mother; I sought to provide her with a narrative that was not wholly foreign. She will never read this, nor would I force her. Between us there remains a desire for the man I called my father; what the exact contours of this desire involve I do not, may not ever, fully know.

I am chasing after uncertain myths, fragments of songs that no one sings. A search for the mythical African phallus.

What constitutes
Silence amidst
These multitudes
Of Stories

:It is said that a Mugikuyu's penis is so large that he wraps it around his waist to carry it:

:It is said that he will sometimes unfurl his penis in the forest and wait for some unsuspecting person to play with it:

:it is said

## Notes

1  I take this title from a discussion held during Jomo Kenyatta's trial, during which he was asked to gloss a curse he had used against the Mau Mau: '*Ngai Mau Mau Irothie Na Miri Ya Mikongoe Yehere Bururi biui biui*' (Slater 156). Literally, the curse consigns the Mau Mau to the roots (*miri*) of a fictional tree (*mikongoe*). Kenyatta glossed it as the 'roots of the unknown'.
2  Readers of Gikuyu will note that I use multiple forms of orthography.
3  I adapt this story from 'Airitu na Irimu' recounted by Njoroge wa Kabugiyo in *Gikuyu Oral Literature*. I have removed diacritical marks that guide pronunciation.

## Works Cited

Barthes, Roland. *Roland Barthes*. Trans. Richard Howard. New York: H.H. and Wang, 1977.
Foucault, Michel. *The History of Sexuality Volume One. An Introduction*. Trans. Robert Hurley. New York: Vintage, 1978.
Freud, Sigmund. *The Interpretation of Dreams*. Trans. James Strachey. New York: Avon, 1965.
Jabes, Edmund. *The Book of Dialogue*. Trans. Rosmarie Waldrop. CT: Wesleyan UP, 1987.
Kabetū, Matthew Njoroge. *Kīrīra Kīa ūgīkūyū* [*Kikuyu: Customs and Traditions of the Kikuyu People*]. Nairobi: EALB, 1947.

Kabira, Wanjiku Mukabi and Karega Mutahi, eds. *Gikuyu Oral Literature*. Nairobi: East African Educational Publishers, 1988.

Nietzsche, Frederick. *On the Advantage and Disadvantage of History for Life*. Trans. Peter Preuss. Indiana: Hacket, 1980.

Slater, Montagu. *The Trial of Jomo Kenyatta*. London: Secker & Warburg, 1955.

Wa Thiong'o, Ngugi. *Matigari ma Njiruungi*. Nairobi: East African Educational Publishers, 1986.

# Ian Iqbal Rashid

## Memory of Fingertips

*for my grandmother*

### 1

Her life got by our clamour, our urgent building, like the narrowest little river slips through a city.

I have a photograph of her gazing at a departure (perhaps my own) as if it were a horizon. (*A horizon is a lie*, I learned later.) It was a time of leavings, of sadness. A time of resignation as she was left behind. But there is an alert stillness that I see in the photos now, a tension found in explorers about to begin their own journeys. She was leaving, going someplace without me. And there was no sadness there, not exactly, just *how to find a way to say goodbye*?

### 2

Photographs: that last one with her arms folded, like she was just about to step back inside (even though we were inside, posing in the recycled warmth of a shopping mall). Her chapped lips seem to tear apart rather than separate, her eyes show an underlay of gold, like sunlight through brown water. How strange she looks, in front of that photographer's fancy backdrop — the humble faded presence of someone known, someone from home.

Then there are the other pictures: a tiny, sickle shaped girl, her head covered. Pretty, vivid, the one you looked at first. More and more pictures, scattered moments attempting to sum up a life. Her faces dissolve and reappear, new selves take shape, rising up to me in degrees, becoming solid. But I know her true face, her final face. The one she was aiming for, the one that

wasn't photographed. All hollow and sharpened — a stark, bare shaving of grey.

Why is this mourning not dangerously slivered? Why no rush toward forgetfulness, that hurried leap past grief? That need to say goodbye with so much feeling that your voice breaks.

### 3

*Our home is a melting smell* she would say and I feel something clench inside her like a deep, internal grip. *Wild oceans swept up to the places we called home.* What must she think of my home, I wonder? A thin city propped up on a lake as flat and pale as paper. Or in the winter: an arty scrawl of black against white.

We leave one morning for the doctor's. I make her go back to change, find something to keep her legs warm. (Nothing about the hard bright light told her it would be cold.) She returns with her legs encased in white nylon stockings beneath her skirt. The wind blows hard, occasionally revealing a frosty sheen like the bloom on a plum.

Back home everything she touched moved off in galloping directions. All her gestures roped in with confidence. The move to every word certain, not yet bridled by English. And now she creaks forward in jagged diagonals, I think, unsure as she clasps my hand.

But at the doctor's, after hours of searching, for words that defy translation, for ailments that can't be located, when I ask her to end a complicated form with an 'x', a smile appears like a lightening rod. She winks and offers the surprise of a signature. I expect a gnarled crumple — but her names, when

*Wasafiri Vol. 22, No. 1 March 2007, pp. 50–51*
ISSN 0269-0055 print/ISSN 1747-1508 online © 2007 Ian Iqbal Rashid
http://www.tandf.co.uk/journals   DOI: 10.1080/02690050601097658

they come, are rounded and curly: balloons anchored at magical angles to one another.

4

What did she make of the century's transformations? What did she make of her own?

I think now of those science-class words, words that meant absence of movement, paralysis. *People stayed where they were.*

During a later visit she reaches up to tousle my hair, but I am not there the way she remembers. Her fingertips want hair falling softly over eyes, a long thickness, a soft-sheen that she wants to press with her palm. She is remembering a boy who lurched among chair legs like a brightly coloured top. A boy who aroused bearded chuckles and crinkled scolding.

On the phone, over the crackle of a bad line she tells me to come home and visit her. (*Home*, she said.) That she no longer remembers who to picture when she speaks to me. *Home*, she said, and *people stayed where they were.*

What did she make of my movements, my crowded life hurtling forward, too unstable for her to climb onto? How was she able to confirm my outline in the blur, to hold me, to ease pain she couldn't even name? Appearing from behind gauze curtains that look like bandages she would know I was awake, just from the bated quality to the air, a clumsy adult man feigning sleep. How did she manage that thin sweet toneless hum no louder than a purr, to place comfort beside me like the curl of a warm cat. To softly shut the door behind her with such care that every hinge, every part of the latch creaked a whispered *I know.*

5

Her room seems drained of colour as if it has already slipped into the dimmest reaches of memory. Even outside, the buildings are so faded they seem hand-tinted.

Death had pushed her hard in the end. Like waves that had rolled her forward, one wave after another, that came closer and closer together. These deaths never left her, *what kind of a mother outlives her children,* but finally allowed her to balance on a narrow surface, allowed her to live there inches above the sadness.

I sit here like she must have done, pressing fingertips to lips. The plaintive wail of a Hindi film song is trampled by the outside traffic. Inside, the elaborate filling of white hours, the glad pounce upon the most inconsequential task. Oceans of chatter and photographs eddy around us.

*That was the song that played at my sister's wedding in 1963,* someone says. And *she wore that sweater when she came to Canada, I sent it to her from England in 19 . . . It must have been 1971.* Gloves. Her hands were badly callused, probably for most of her life. *I remember them against my fevered forehead,* her cool and definite fingertips.

Fingertips. How to live free in a world where the passing of time holds such power?

# Ruth Vanita and Saleem Kidwai in Conversation

**Gautam Bhan**

Although many battles remain for queer people in India, newly confident gay, lesbian, bisexual and transgendered communities have emerged over the past decade. Meanwhile, Indian publishing houses – who nearly a decade ago maintained a stony silence when it came to sexuality – are eager to print books on queer lives. To understand these changes in attitude, it is important to scrutinise how sexuality is being written about in fiction, popular writing and the Indian academy. What are publishers willing to print, and what are bookstores willing to stock? To discuss these issues, I caught up with Saleem Kidwai and Ruth Vanita on a breezy New Delhi evening in September 2006.

Saleem Kidwai taught Indian medieval history for nearly twenty years at the University of Delhi. He has long been associated with the gay rights movement in India, helping to establish some of the earliest gay support spaces in Delhi. Kidwai is also a scholar of Urdu literature and has translated the famous ghazal singer Malika Pukhraj's autobiography, entitled Song Sung True, into English. Kidwai is based in Lucknow.

Ruth Vanita is the author of Love's Rite: Same-Sex Marriage in India and the West (Penguin, 2006) and is currently Professor of Liberal Studies and Women's Studies at the University of Montana. She taught at Delhi University for many years, where she was founding co-editor of Manushi women's magazine from 1978 to 1990. Her other publications include Sappho and the Virgin Mary: Same Sex Love and the English Literary Imagination (1996), editing Queering India (2002) and the English translation of a Hindi novel by Rajendra Yadav, Strangers on the Roof (1994). Her collected essays, Gandhi's Tiger and Sita's smile, came out recently.

Ruth Vanita and Saleem Kidwai have been key figures in engineering the current trend of openness towards writing on same-sex desire in India and co-edited the groundbreaking book Same-Sex Love in India: Readings from Literature and History (Palgrave Macmillan, 2001). Spanning many centuries of Indian history and numerous linguistic traditions, the volume brings together diverse texts that uncover stories of same-sex love. This text has been seminal in beginning the shift to queer-positive representations in Indian writing and shatters the myth that homosexuality is traditionally not a part of subcontinental culture and history.

**Gautam Bhan** So, Saleem and Ruth, where did the idea of Same-Sex Love in India come from? What was the journey to edit and publish it like?

**Ruth Vanita** We had independently been collecting materials on homosexuality in India for many years before the project began. But to me, it had earlier seemed too daunting to do alone. The idea of writing the book together came in 1994. We drew up a list of writings we already knew about, and started looking for other material.

**GB** Who did you take the project to at this stage? Were there people willing to publish it?

**Saleem Kidwai** We went to Columbia University Press because Ruth knew the editor there, who liked our project. Readers gave excellent responses to our proposal. We worked with the editor there for a year on it, and she shaped the book in many ways. One of the things she said was that she didn't want any homophobic writing in it.

**GB** Did she give a reason for not wanting homophobic writing?

**SK** She felt that since it was the first book of its kind at a time when there wasn't much, if any, writing on homosexuality out there ... we should focus on the positive. Both of us were a little uncomfortable with that. She left Columbia then, and the new editor there didn't want the book. So we shifted to St Martin's, where we were open to including all kinds of texts. I think the book does clearly have an emphasis on the positive. But we didn't want to completely ignore relatively negative writing. We had to acknowledge how homophobic narratives have played a part in the history of writing about homosexuality in India. With important writers, the choice to write about homosexuality, regardless of their judgments of it, has an importance.

Wasafiri Vol. 22, No. 1 March 2007, pp. 52–56

ISSN 0269-0055 print/ISSN 1747-1508 online © 2007 Wasafiri
http://www.tandf.co.uk/journals    DOI: 10.1080/02690050601097674

We realise in retrospect that we were then on the verge of a new phase of gay writing when the book got published. Before us, there were only two serious books — by Rakesh Ratti and Giti Thadani. Ratti's book – *A Lotus of Another Colour* – sort of hung in the air. There was simply no history or community for it to stand on. Ashwini Sukthankar's *Facing the Mirror: Lesbian Writing in India* came a year after ours. Each book has built a readership and a community since then.

**GB** As people who write on sexuality in the Indian context, how do we decide what to put out there as a representation of ourselves? When Arvind Narrain and I were doing our anthology *Because I Have a Voice*, there was a very conscious sense that we wanted a strong community voice to emerge. Not that we wanted a consensus or for no negative experiences told, but the one thing we told our writers was to reflect from positions of strength. We wanted to send a message that queer people, no matter what they have gone through, are out there and have made their lives work. I feel like that did colour our selection process. In a sense, it was not so much about simply putting out a book, but it was almost as if we were trying to build a community. We were very unapologetic about that.

You told me once that eighty per cent of the original material you had was not included in the final book. In the process of choosing the twenty per cent that made it, did you have a certain type of representation already in mind? Certain kinds of writing and histories on sexuality you thought you wanted people to know about more critically than others? I suppose what I'm asking is, how are we to go about choosing representations when these representations really are the first works that are building queer discourse in India?

**SK** Ultimately, that's how we did decide. We thought about pieces that we really wanted people to know about. We had so much more material than we bargained for.

**RV** We did not only look for self-identified queer writers. We looked for important, interesting and moving texts in a wide range of genres. Almost all of the material included was already published. Many pieces were part of the canon but had never been looked at from the perspective of sexuality, or are small pieces of writing that have been overlooked because they are placed in the middle of larger works. Our purpose was to examine the history of ideas, the history of the discussion in India on the theme of same-sex relationships. Since the texts are about same-sex love, we were looking for difference. But we found that it's not only present at the margins. Many canonical writers have written about same-sex desire, and we chose to highlight that. We also took a decision to use less of the writing we had in English because it is already accessible, writers like Suniti Namjoshi, for example. Or Raj Rao, Firdaus Kanga, Aubrey Menen. We wanted to emphasise writing in Indian languages to pointedly counter the myth that homosexuality is a Western construction. To that end, and for the accessibility reasons, we used very little writing in English, though we have a small lesser known poem by Vikram Seth.

**SK** This is still a work in progress. There is so much more there in the languages we have covered, and also languages in which we were not able to get any sources — Telugu for one, and Assamese and other North-eastern languages. We haven't done nearly enough research in this area.

**GB** What then about the understanding of sexuality in itself? One of the hardest things to do in choosing to write and represent sexuality is to choose a working definition of what we mean by sexuality. Is it sexual identity? Contemporary language and politics give us so many terms and identifiers — Lesbian, Gay, Bisexual, Transgendered [LGBT]. I'm constantly told that there isn't enough gay fiction and am always struck by what people consider as 'gay' fiction. Identity seems to play such a central role. When Maya Sharma's recent work – *Loving Women: Being Lesbian in Unpriviliged India,* which compiles oral histories of women loving women in working class, small town and rural contexts – came out, she had a lovely piece about the difficulty of using the word 'lesbian' when many of the women she talked about didn't use it themselves, and where many of the histories in that book were almost about fleeting moments and unfinished stories that didn't fall easily into a narrative of a 'queer' life. When looking at a time when identity labels didn't exist for the most part, how did you to decide about an appropriate manner to write about sexuality? And how do you think your work converges or diverges with contemporary sexual politics?

**SK** I think the basis for us was love and not sexuality alone.

**RV** We could have titled the book 'Same-Sex Desire', for instance. Or 'Same-Sex Sexuality'. But we chose 'Love'.

**SK** Our focus was love, given that the span of material and the nature of it ... was so varied — over two thousand years and different languages and genres of writing. It was love between the same sex that became our thumb rule. It became the lens that explained all the variations.

**RV** We found that love was a flexible enough concept. It can include sexuality but is not limited to it, or to one understanding of it. It can be erotic, romantic, intimate and sexual in different senses.

**SV** We don't know if, or are not even suggesting, that sex occurred between the protagonists in our stories. We aren't even saying that the writers were gay or lesbian themselves. I don't think that matters.

**RV** Several pioneering Gay Studies researchers from the 1970s onwards, like Lillian Faderman, Carroll Smith-Rosenberg and John Boswell, have pointed out that what is important in looking at history is the intensity and passion of a same-sex relationship, not whether particular genital acts took place. I think it is established now that it's not the sex act that is so important to capture. This is already the case with heterosexuals. Take the case of Romeo and Juliet. No one would say that their love is defined by sex acts.

**GB** But you don't think that there is this pressure or a need that says that we need to call these writings LGBT? That the contemporary moment wishes to say these are gay writers writing for gay people?

**RV** I think that's fine in the present moment but it cannot easily be imported into the past. I don't think it's wrong to want queer-identified literature, but that's not the only important literature on same-sex relations.

**GB** But do we think that what we've got is representative? That it is the kind of writing that people want to read?

**SK** What we want is good writing more than simply any gay writing. I don't think there is a shortage of gay writing, but why would I read bad gay writing? I'm not at a point now when I need the basics to feel validated as gay or Indian. Now I want good writing. There was a point when no publisher wanted us. Now everyone does. I think editors are kinder when the subject is LGBT and publish bad writing. I think there was a time when the need for representation overtook the importance of how good the work was. I think we're past that today. What I want to see is good research or good creative writing. It doesn't matter how the author identifies.

**RV** I think what matters is that the text speaks to you. Vikram Chandra's *Red Earth and Pouring Rain* has a story about two men, and Vijay Dan Detha has a wonderful story about two women. And as far as I know, both authors are straight men. I wouldn't necessarily know the author's sexual identity when I pick up the book. In the case of the past, we certainly don't know what the authors were. It doesn't matter. What is important is that writers write about same-sex love sensitively, and that readers are moved by it.

**GB** Do you see a change in the tone of writing today?

**SK** I think the biggest change is in newspaper writing, actually. There was never the breadth nor the kind of writing that we see today.

**RV** Yes. In the 1970s and early 1980s, whatever was published was almost all about the West. Reports about what was happening there. And this fed the idea of homosexuality being Western. Now almost every day, there are reports or mentions of homosexuality in Indian media.

**SK** And even the tone of the writing. It shows a receptivity. I think this is the time for good creative fiction to be written. The audience is there, and the media are willing to write about it. Look at Abha Dawesar. Could she have been published ten years ago? *Same-Sex Love* was published through the back door by Macmillan India who publish textbooks because no mainstream publisher would publish us. They did nothing to distribute it or promote it. It was bookstores who would harass them because people were asking. And this was after we had been published abroad with good reviews and no controversy. Today the book is in demand and is going to be reissued by Penguin.

**GB** But do you think there still remains a difference when it comes from major publishing houses? We know that bookstores are still hesitant to take books that are open about sexuality when they don't come under big publishing brands. For example, with *Because I Have a Voice,* we found that bookstores were happy to carry it once the *Hindustan Times* and *Times of India* had carried reviews. These reviews gave the book legitimacy. Do you think we should take this seriously as one of the reasons why we in India don't have more people – gay or straight – writing about sexuality, and especially writing popular fiction?

**RV** I don't think that's a barrier. I think bookstores are willing to carry any book that they think will sell.

**SK** Books also always appear in stages. People will store books that will sell. I'm closely associated with a bookstore in a small town. I know that the only copies left of *Same-Sex Love in India* are now with that small town bookstore because it's out of print, and that's where people order it from now, at a higher price. It's interesting, the book is selling more now than it was in the middle period — something which is indicative of a change. I think the life of a book cannot be judged within a year or two years of its birth.

**GB** So you don't think there is a hesitancy on the part of bookstores in keeping books on homosexuality?

**SK** I don't think there is a bias.

**RV** They'll look at the cover, the title, what is marketable. It's about what they think will sell.

**GB** Ruth, your new book, *Love's Rite*, is sold as a general release. The coffee shop next to my office has it in its display case. Bookstores have a way of taking the 'academic' titles and putting them in a dark corner. But this book is not positioned that way. Was that intentional? Do you think it's given you a different readership and had a different impact because of that positioning?

**RV** I think I've always aspired to write in a way that is accessible to the general reader. This aspiration developed when I worked at *Manushi* [a journal of Women's Studies in India], and maybe it's only now that I've succeeded. I wanted to take complex ideas and make them simple. In *Same-Sex Love*, we were trying to do just that. I'm always surprised that people find it scholarly and daunting. *Love's Rite* is different also because it is largely about the contemporary, and many people prefer to read about the present, not the past.

**GB** What made you write about same-sex marriage? The dominant trope in writing about homosexuality in India has been confined to personal narratives, and quite often to stories about how hard that life is. No one, really, has written about marriage.

**RV** It's entirely triggered for me by the stories of poor and lower middle-class young female couples since 1980 who have been getting married, often with religious rites, often with the support of their families in small towns. And many others have committed joint suicide, which I read as a type of marriage. To me, it's one of the most interesting same-sex phenomena in the twentieth century, and in India. It's also strikingly different from the West. Coming out narratives in India are not that different from such narratives in the West. A boy coming out in rural Montana, or one coming out in a small town in North India, like Meerut — there are certain similarities. You feel like you're the only one in the world, and then you find community and grow confident. But marrying by Hindu ceremonies, and also the many cases of joint suicides – where women have killed themselves rather than be separated – are unique phenomena. You have individual suicides in the West, but not many joint suicides. And this phenomenon of it happening again and again in India suggests that it is a pattern rooted in history and tradition. Most importantly, these unions occur entirely outside the gay movement, which had no grasp of the phenomenon, analysis of it or contact with it. To me, the gay movement in India, despite all the differences, is not radically and entirely different from movements in the West.

I have been intrigued and moved by these unions for decades, collecting news reports of them. And I've been unable to explain them, especially why some families were supportive. There is something in some traditions, some families and some communities, that makes it possible to accept these relationships. And what is that? I think it's really important to find out what makes acceptance possible. What makes marriage possible in one context and only suicide possible in another? In the course of this research, I also came to see many similarities between the supposedly mainstream heterosexual and the supposedly marginal homosexual. Looking at two girls or a boy/girl couple, if the suicide notes are pretty much the same, the suicides are in defiance of the family and authorities. Both are focused on the refusal to be separated. Now it's up to me. I could ignore the heterosexual ones as some writers about lesbian suicides have, and focus only on the lesbian ones to prove that only lesbians are oppressed in this way. But I think this would be doing an injustice. I think it's also useful to acknowledge similarities rather then only emphasise differences. In similar situations, human beings react similarly.

**GB** Is that the thinking also behind translating Ugra? In this last project, Ruth, you took a Hindi writer from the early part of the twentieth century who wrote these stories that, according the author himself, were intended to expose and eradicate homosexuality. Though you argue in your translation that Ugra unwittingly also gave a language and expression to homosexuality despite his intentions, did you feel a sense of trepidation about putting such stories back into circulation in a society that remains largely homophobic? Where many people could in fact agree with Ugra's point of view?

**SK** We found Ugra late in our research. We had a chapter on him in *Same-Sex Love* as well. But we thought it was very important to show that, in certain periods, homophobia was the only mode in which one could speak about homosexuality. There is an Urdu critic, Shadani, who has combed the poetry of Ghalib to point out any instances, no matter how small, of boy love, and said, 'These should be purged.' It's interesting that he made the effort of looking and finding all these references, which he needn't have done to make his point. Now these stand as a really important archive for those working on sexuality from a completely different ideological viewpoint. For me, it says a lot that he made that effort. He devoted all his time to this subject though he thinks it's perverse!

**GB** You think that there is readership that is ready to receive such texts and not read them simplistically?

**RV** I think that this readership existed even then. I first found out about Ugra's *Chocolate* when gay activist Ashok Row Kavi told me that an older gay man, a contemporary of Ugra, told him that gay men had been really excited about the release of Ugra's stories. Despite his negative tone, he wrote about homosexuality explicitly during a time when there was nothing else there. In fact, his critics accused him of writing in a way that made it seem very attractive, even though the characters often met catastrophic ends to make a moral point. So it is not just we today reading it subversively. Some readers read it that way in its own time. I don't think we should underestimate the possibility of different types of readings in any period.

**SK** There was a Marathi writer who did something very similar. The homosexuals in his stories always met terrible ends. But

there was such detail about gay life and the cruising scene in Bombay that somehow it felt like an insider's view of what was happening. At a certain point in history, negative writing was the only way to write about it. For us, readership wasn't an issue, we were trying to document our history.

**GB** Do you think, though, that the book actually has been read more widely than one would imagine? That despite what Ruth said earlier about it being seen as academic and scholarly, it has become this work that everyone talks about in very different circles, including popular ones? It seems to have a status that other kinds of academic books just don't have.

**RV** I have heard stories about this. A friend's boss — a regular middle-class man with no real interest in history — picked it up from her desk, read it and was impressed by it.

**SK** It has had a very wide and interesting reception in academia, and it is cited so widely. But I do think that it has been ignored by the gay community. People still tell me today that they've just discovered that Babar had a lover or the writings of Mir, and they act so surprised. So clearly the book hasn't reached a large gay readership in India, and that has been very disappointing for me. I thought gay people were waiting for this history. My need to write that book was to write my own history. All those years teaching history and you realise that the only history you can't write is your own.

**GB** What do you think explains this neglect by India's gay readers?

**SK** I think part of it is the time in which the book was released. There wasn't any kind of distribution or marketing, and the media weren't writing openly and positively about it. The kind of infrastructure we have to write about sexuality today wasn't there. I'm hoping that the second reprint will change all that.

**GB** Here's hoping that's true!

# Jackie Kay

## Facing the Double Bed, Single

You take the risk and leave your other half.
Things tremble in the balance.
You are in two minds, unsure which way to jump.
You close the door and move into the grey area,
the limbo land between your past and future.

Time apart is a leap in the dark.
You have no idea where you are headed for.
For a while you live on the qui vive,
Blow hot and cold, play fast and loose.
At night, you stare at the wall for an age.

Your double bed is a ship in the dark.
A lighthouse light twirls to keep you safe.
You tell yourself you have been brave.
You clung on for dear life; it was a near thing.
You were on the slippery slope.

When the fog lifts you'll see things clearly.

*Wasafiri Vol. 22, No. 1 March 2007, p. 57*
ISSN 0269-0055 print/ISSN 1747-1508 online © 2007 Wasafiri
http://www.tandf.co.uk/journals    DOI: 10.1080/02690050601097682

Routledge
Taylor & Francis Group

# Blue Women

## Gillian Hanscombe

Jonquil was no flower, though her mother had fervently wished it. Her mother, big and bony, wearer of sensible shoes and large flowing smocks, had spent her early life answering to Louisa, which in adult life she contracted to Lou, but in her mind there was nothing petite about either. She harboured secret longings for a pretty girl-child, a dainty dancer, or a pert little miss who could be dressed in party frocks and have her fine hair shaped with combs and ribbons. Wilfully pregnant at a young age, and even more wilfully determined to see what she could of the world as it was then, Lou booked a berth on a cargo ship taking a few passengers to the East: the Maldives, India, the South China Sea. Once boarded, she kept herself to herself, read books, studied maps and travel guides, stared at the cresting waves, and talked to the child growing within her. If the others — crew or fellow passengers alike — found her strange and remote, it bothered her not at all. All she wanted of human company was already inside her and all she had to do was wait.

For Lou, alone and happy, the sights and smells of India were astonishing, intoxicating, unprecedented. She must stay. There was no other option. She could teach English somewhere, or look after the children of rich Westerners, or be a receptionist in a hotel or large company — something would be possible in such a dense tapestry, such a teeming bazaar of human ingenuity and exchange. And it wasn't difficult. There was a wealthy Hindu family who wanted an English tutor for their children, and because she was white and foreign, they made no mention of her coming child except to clarify her terms and conditions of employment and ensure that the educational needs of their own children should have prior claims on her time. Lou was sensible. Lou was capable. She could manage everything easily. Her baby, when she came, would not be neglected. Lou was sure about everything, even her conviction that her baby was a daughter. At night before sleeping she imagined the party frocks to be bought, the bangles and necklaces, maybe some ballet shoes if a teacher could be found. Lou feared nothing: life flowed like a river, strong and unceasing, and she flowed in its current, watching and seeing, listening, absorbing, willing what she knew to flow into her womb, into her quiet daughter.

The birth when it came was unproblematic and caused no sensation. Indeed the baby was a girl, as she'd known it would be; and there were no adverse signs of any kind, neither physical nor psychic, nor elemental, nor even practical. Her employers allowed Lou her two weeks' annual leave, and she learned her daughter's look and feel, her skin, her downy scalp, her tiny nails, her violet-coloured eyes. The two, mother and daughter, lay in bed, sucking and sleeping, eating, cuddling, bathing, crooning. It was as it was. Lou named her baby Jonquil, seeing what she had always wished to see: a spring bloom, a fresh and female fountain, a tiny force, a flower.

Though born and brought up in India, Jonquil was not, of course, Indian — well, not visibly, that is. What no one knew about, not even her mother (who otherwise seemed always to know everything) was her friendship with Lord Krishna. She had always known him, in her earliest memories, in her first dreams. He spoke to her as normally and naturally as anyone spoke to her, though she knew, without knowing how, that no one else could hear or observe his presence. She had never been afraid of the god, since his company was always warm and constant. It is possible that her unusual serenity, her calm, her confidence, flowed from this friendship, though observers — knowing nothing of that — put it down to her mother's devotion. Either way, Jonquil was a great success as her mother's daughter, except for her large frame: clearly, by the age of four, even Lou had to admit that party frocks and beribboned hairstyles made Jonquil look a fright. It's my fault, thought Lou sadly: no one can fight genes.

All went well. Days passed, years passed. Until Jonquil turned thirteen and the changes in her body began to make her head swim. The colours around her darkened and glowed; the savour of food grew more intense; the air she breathed thickened with import, meaning, exchange, relationship of

*Wasafiri Vol. 22, No. 1 March 2007, pp. 58–60*
ISSN 0269-0055 print/ISSN 1747-1508 online © 2007 Gillian Hanscombe
http://www.tandf.co.uk/journals    DOI: 10.1080/02690050601097690

person to person, person to creature, creature to environment. The brilliance of things dazzled her; the raucousness deafened her; the passage from waking to sleeping, thinking to dreaming, turned seamless. When she fell in love, the drumming of blood in her ears and thighs felt utterly inevitable. Lord Krishna commiserated, soothed, murmured ancient songs that lilted through her broken thoughts like honey through dry bread. Her love was unattainable: her love was called Shobhana, tall and lithe, and all of seventeen. Shobhana was a daughter of friends of Lou's employers; she was due to be married to a minor aristocrat from one of the former princely states, and the preparations were long and complex. Jonquil gazed and suffered, yearned and dreamed, and Lord Krishna whispered his reassurances.

The first kiss was unexpected, the two moving simultaneously together in an empty corridor outside the kitchen. The servants were sleeping following the midday meal, and the adults were sequestered with their planning lists and schedules. – I never imagined ... began Jonquil (though of course she had imagined, often); but Shobhana said – Don't speak; don't say anything at all ... and laid on Jonquil's lips her own moist, luscious, questing open mouth. What followed seemed effortless: assignations, hours and half-hours quickly plotted, beds, divans, even cupboards found instantly, agreeably, while servants toiled elsewhere and the adults talked and planned.

Lou felt troubled by Jonquil's new evasiveness but put it down to adolescent moods, flighty interests, normal growing up. The wedding, after all, was the centre-piece of the household's preoccupations. Shobhana was a beautiful girl, thought Lou: she deserved the best celebration possible. Sadly, in comparison, she thought of her own ungainly girl, wondered what would become of her, considered for the thousandth time whether she should take them both to England, but rejected the thought in a panic of memories — the grey days, the brutality, the ugly housing sprawl, the drone of politicians on television. At least in India everything was possible, by virtue of the multiplicities of style and system, history, hope, and indefatigable industriousness.

There was a year of preparation and planning for the wedding. Jonquil turned fourteen. Her breasts grew larger, she gained two inches in height, and lost some puppy fat. Love-making with Shobhana became even more voluptuous, the rhythms and exertions patterned and extended through practice and confidence. The wet limbs, shining eyes, squelch and suck of skin and orifice were in themselves hypnotic — and overriding all, like a caressing whisper, was the sound of the thin high flute of Lord Krishna, fountain of light and love.

Time flowed, and the wedding took place as it should and must, according to custom and expectation. What could otherwise disrupt the fabric of being and doing so anciently established? Nothing essential, that is, was changed. The new husband Vikram was hardly more than a boy, smooth-cheeked and impetuous, keen on sports, cars, and the gentler versions of nightlife. Because of Shobhana's pleadings, but also because it was convenient for everybody, it was agreed

that the pair would live in an apartment in Shobhana's family home. Vikram's father was a widower with many women friends, and Shobhana's mother was not yet ready to let her daughter go.

Vikram's father ran a medium-sized export business dealing in budget exotica for European markets: soapstone boxes, silver jewellery, brassware, monkeys and elephants in wood and bone, all manner of machine-embroidered cushion covers and other practical fabrics. Vikram had a desk, a phone, some office equipment and a secretary in his father's premises. He was learning the business. He was, predictably enough, a very part-time learner, but he was young, his father was still vigorous, and the flow of time and money in such an environment were unimpeded by the frivolities of youth. The marriage with Shobhana, like similar marriages, was quiet and easy. They played their parts and continued on their separate ways, waiting for the first pregnancy to announce itself.

Lord Krishna also seemed to wait, soothing Jonquil with music from his flute when she lay alone, longing for Shobhana; and whispering delights when the two women dreamed in each other's arms after lovemaking. At first Jonquil's anxieties were great: what will happen? What will happen? she asked. The answer, coming through flute and whisper, became reassuring with repetition: it is always like this. It is always like this.

Nothing changed. In time, Shobhana and Vikram produced three babies. Jonquil was wooed, now and then, by Western men with money who liked a challenge, and Indian men rebelling against traditional expectations. She dallied and parried, enjoyed the attention, reassured her mother, helped with Shobhana's babies, and considered whether or not to train in teaching or child management. It would be possible for her to avoid marriage altogether, just as her mother had. Lord Krishna listened, nodded, understood, encouraged. He would protect her. She would be faithful.

It's said that in the Indian languages there is no word for lesbian. That is because women's secrets lie buried within walls and alcoves, within silks and linens, between the looks and whispers of women secluded away from men and money, public affairs, laws and policies. Lord Krishna, however, presides and protects. He covers women's lovemaking with whispers and fluteplaying. He keeps in his bosom all that has passed between women from the beginning of the world. This knowledge is what turned his skin blue, long ago — the blue of sky and ocean, river, lake and magical flower, the blue of infinite congress, signifying renewal. He allows men to marvel at his range of seductions, knowing them to be too worldly to be able to interpret. Women know better the nature and degree of his dominion.

Marriage might be successfully avoided, agreed Lou, but only via a formal training, there being no savings to speak of. It was reasonable. Three years in the West at an approved institution of some kind could secure her independence. When Jonquil turned twenty-one, Lord Krishna laid his flute aside and spoke to her clearly, in English. – Soon you will be in England for your university training. You have been faithful to me and I owe you one wish. Consider carefully. I promise I will fulfil what you ask, whatever you ask. Jonquil smiled. She had read extensively and knew the pitfalls of asking the gods for long life or wealth, happiness, children, success, or any kind of charmed life. She lived in India, after all: there was devastation everywhere.

One week later, after much speculation, after dreaming and imagining, she gave her reply. – I would like, she requested Lord Krishna – I would like you to turn my skin blue like yours; and not only mine, but Shobhana's; and not only hers, but the skin of every woman in the world whose desire for women is like ours. We would then know one another at a glance. And we would belong to you openly.

Lord Krishna smiled. – You hardly know what you ask, he murmured. – Don't you realise by now that the majority of women are just like you and Shobhana? Don't you know that what flows between you flows from me? Flows towards all women? Flows between them and me? You would have nearly half the people in the world coloured blue.

Jonquil considered. She thought and sighed. And then she dreamed. She dreamed the dream of Lord Krishna in his chariot, contemplating destiny. – Let it be, she breathed. – Let it be as you have intended. When I am in England surrounded by everything alien, let me wear the blue of sky and ocean,

the blue of your blessing. Let me think of Shobhana here with you, with her blue skin smooth and outspoken, within the range of your music. Let me see in my dreams the women of the world encompassed by your breathing.

The god meditated for a long time. Then smiled again. – But what of the enmity of the patriarchs? reasoned Lord Krishna. – And the enmity of their women, who have chosen to evade my embraces and to shut out my music? They are also considerable in number. Is it not better to keep hidden the true secrets of women's desire for each other? Is it really your wish that everything be uncovered? Will you exchange what is easy and blissful for ignominy and confrontation?

Jonquil, grown suddenly beautiful from Lord Krishna's gaze, remembering her mother's courage and devotion, remembering Shobhana's birthpains, remembering the sculptures of the dance scattered the length and breadth of India, remembering the flute music that had played through all her memories, right from the beginning, began to assemble gifts of incense and fruit, milk and flowers, for the honour of the god.

– Let it be as I have dreamed, she whispered. – When I am finally in England, let it be as I have dreamed.

# 'If You Like Professor, I Will Come Home With You'

## A RE-READING OF WOLE SOYINKA'S THE ROAD

**Chris Dunton**

Homoeroticism, same-sex sexual desire and/or experience of gay identity, have hardly featured prominently as subject matter in Soyinka's writing or public statements. Aside from a handful of circumspect comments in interview – for example, on Mugabe's homophobia – and some incidental references in texts such as *Season of Anomy* or *A Play of Giants*, the one extended treatment of this field of cognition and experience in Soyinka's work lies in his characterisation of the African American gay man Joe Golder in the novel *The Interpreters* (for a detailed examination of this, see Hoad).

In advocating a reading of Professor, the central character in Soyinka's play *The Road*, as a figure attracted to other men, I am not suggesting that homosexual orientation or desire were in Soyinka's mind when he conceived the play — or, at least, not to the forefront of his mind. I am taking my cue, rather, from Harold Bloom's notion of a 'strong reading', that is, a 'misreading' of a text that brings out features and qualities in a work that have previously lain dormant or have been marginalised by hegemonic readings. It was this kind of reading that I attempted in an essay titled 'Back on *The Road* again; Soyinka's Professor and *Vodou*'s Baron Samedi', when I suggested parallels (in dress, habitat, conduct) between Professor and *Vodou*'s Lord of the Cemetery and between Professor's relationships with the inhabitants of the motor-park and the Baron's relationships with his 'clientele' and with the *zombi*. It is this notion that provides for the intention of the present essay: to suggest a reading of Professor as queer holds promise for a staging of the play that would cast fresh light on the motivations for his actions and the needs and emotions underpinning his relationships with the other characters. The suggestion was that,

> while *The Road* has always been credited with a high degree of polysemy – that is, the bearing of multiple

interpretations – it may be a little more polysemic, even, than we thought. (Dunton 16)

Cheerfully mindful of the fact that, as Derek Wright puts it, 'mountains of exegesis' have already been heaped upon *The Road* (89), the present paper attempts to expand the existing repertoire of interpretation of the play by adding one item (though this is an interpretation intended to augment rather than supplant available readings). Starting-points in this instance include: a re-reading of the play text; memories of Femi Osofisan's 1990 production of the play at the University of Ibadan (seen by me on its 1993 revival); Osofisan's programme note, which speaks of the way that 'masochism, violence and crime' intersect in the milieu of the motor-park (the single, paradoxically claustrophobic, setting for the play); and a conviction that, with the character of Professor in mind, we can readily add 'sadism' to Osofisan's listing. Another, and a major starting-point is an essay by Biodun Jeyifo entitled 'Whose Theatre, Whose Africa? Wole Soyinka's *The Road* on the Road', which compares three stagings of the play (all outside Africa) and which adopts Harold Bloom's idea (developed in *A Map of Misreading*) of the 'strong reading' as one of its major critical instruments. This application of Bloom's idea has subsequently been taken up by Bernth Lindfors who analysed Soyinka's own 1984 production of *The Road* at the Goodman Theater, Chicago. One of the stagings Jeyifo analyses is Yvonne Brewster's 1992 London production (not seen by me, unfortunately), which reportedly introduced a strongly homoerotic charge to Professor's relationships with the touts, drivers and mechanics who inhabit the motor-park. It is this notion that provides for the intention of the present essay: to propose that a queer reading of Professor holds promise for a vital (but of course by no means uniquely legitimate or plausible) staging of the play which informs my suggestion that a reading of Professor as subject to same-sex desire opens up a new dimension in the staging of the play.

*Wasafiri Vol. 22, No. 1 March 2007, pp. 61–65*

ISSN 0269-0055 print/ISSN 1747-1508 online © 2007 Wasafiri
http://www.tandf.co.uk/journals    DOI: 10.1080/02690050601097732

The extent of the impact that such a reading would have on *The Road* in production depends, clearly, on how central a character Professor is seen to be to the play. On this question Femi Fatoba comments that:

> *The Road* is Professor's play. He is more often than not the topic of discussion. When he is not, he is invited to listen, give an opinion or simply provoked with questions. (67)

Indeed, Soyinka himself has commented: 'The play *is* the Professor . . . the play is about words' (Mike 49). Fatoba notes, too, how Professor 'lives in the privacy of a self-created world' and speaks of the way in which the other characters continually 'dare to step on the edges of his consciousness', and it is this that provokes the seemingly erratic and often irascible nature of his responses to them (66). One could go further and note that time and time again the other characters – Kotonu, Samson and Salubi, especially – grapple to achieve engagement with Professor's consciousness, reaching out to him and then, as often as not, when he responds aggressively or with some alienating, arcane pronouncement, shrinking back. This is less true of Murano, whose relationship with Professor is, while enigmatic, fixed and secure. Yet it would be a mistake to consider these characters as vapid, as mere functions in a play of call and response in which Professor is dominant: they have real and multifarious vitality in themselves. Simon Gikandi has even gone as far as to suggest that anyone who has seen the play will agree that Samson is its major character (24). Consider in contrast Ketu Katrak's view of Soyinka's 1984 Goodman Theater production: 'the layabouts functioned primarily as a silent backdrop . . . only when one of them was talking to Professor . . . did that character come to life on stage', concluding – surely riskily, on the basis of a single production – 'the dramatic structure of *The Road* is much more powerful in the written text than in actualization on stage' (61). Other times, other places, another production, another outcome.

The question as to whether Fatoba's and Gikandi's views can be reconciled depends in part on how much credence one can place on the notion of the 'strong reading' in the context of possible alternative stagings of the play. Certainly in the 1990/ 1993 Osofisan production the characters Samson and Salubi came across with tremendous bearing in regard to their wit, Salubi's combination of insouciance and self-concern, Samson's reflectiveness and solicitousness; further, the chorus of touts, drivers, mechanics and thugs had great physical presence, enabled partly by Osofisan's foregrounding of the series of songs and chants that run throughout the play. In the performances of Say Tokyo Kid and of the lead (and guitar-playing) layabout there was considerable foregrounding of the virility and agility – even the flaunting – of the male body. The effect ranged between the thrilling and the threatening (depending on audience reception) to the simply appealing — as in one scene in which Salubi lay on his back on the ground, tossed groundnuts up in the air and, with considerable skill, caught them in his mouth, a moment that perfectly encapsulated his character. At the same time certain questions could be asked about Femi Fatoba's performance as Professor, an experience that clearly informs his 1996 essay. Fatoba's involvement with the play stretches back over decades – he (as Eddie Fatoba) took part in the play's 1965 premiere at the Theatre Royal, Stratford East in London as a member of the 'music and dance ensemble' (personal communication, Dapo Adelugba to CD, 18 Jan. 2006) – and his unexpectedly low-key interpretation of the main role accentuated the eccentric, even risible aspects of the Professor's behaviour.

One could argue that Fatoba's performance homogenised Soyinka's characterisation of Professor, flattening peaks and troughs and understating the character's volatility. Professor himself asks at one point 'Don't we all change from minute to minute? If we didn't we wouldn't hope to die' (Soyinka 85). The changes in his behaviour towards the other characters are continual and often bewildering to them. He is capable of the most straightforward and reasonable conduct imaginable, for example, in his account of his rescue of Murano (44), and also of the most elusive and arcane. He can engage in a gentle, teasing humour, as when Samson comments on the retirement of the driver Kotonu, 'Look, Professor, the road won't be the same without him', and Professor offers the rejoinder 'He was a road mender too?' (37). He is also capable of chilling threat, as when Samson speculates that he might one day follow Murano on his dawn travels and Professor responds 'You are tired of life perhaps?' (45). Any staged production should surely emphasise this highly disconcerting volatility in Professor's behaviour while also offering the audience some kind of a handle to enable them to grasp why he behaves in this way (what kind of handle would depend on what kind of reading is being attempted).

An initial pointer to the character of Professor – and especially to his 'unreadability' – can be found in 'Alagemo', the poem with which Soyinka prefaces the published play and which dates from at least as early as 1959, when it was performed as part of an evening of poetry and drama by Soyinka at London's Royal Court theatre. The poem is in turn preceded by a note explaining that 'agemo' – from which the word 'alagemo' derives – is 'a religious cult of flesh dissolution' and that the term '"agemo" phase' refers to 'the passage of transition from the human to the divine essence' (Soyinka [ii]). The poem, then, can be taken to refer in the first instance to the experience of the character Murano, knocked down by a motor vehicle during the annual drivers' festival, while performing a masquerade — that is, while making corporeal the recognition of the potentiality of transition.[1] Yet the poem can also be taken to reflect upon Professor, on his quest for an understanding of life and death and of the liminal space within which the two are bound. 'I heard!' the poem begins, 'I felt their reach/And heard my naming named' (Soyinka [iii]).

Throughout the play, Professor seeks the Word — seeks to pin it down, to name the name. While he is very talkative about his self-appointed role, his quest, he is at the same time generally extremely evasive — a rare moment of apparently absolute candour being his admission, following the question 'Don't we all change from minute to minute?' that at a point in his life he has lost his way (Soyinka 85). Mostly he dares not, or at least declines to, speak his name. He is at once remote and massively present — even when physically absent — constituting what Terry Eagleton might refer to as an 'absent centre' (125). He is thus from the very beginning of the play when Samson and Salubi catalogue his personal attributes: he is a 'madman', he sleeps in the cemetery, he may be a millionaire, he is an expert forger of driving licences (4–5). A great deal is known or surmised about him, and yet, behind this whirl of perceptions, he remains essentially unknown.

Samson and Salubi's opening dialogue develops into a role-play episode: as we come to realise in retrospect (for Professor is not yet present on stage) this is a representation of a representation, a quasi-burlesque of Professor's public performance. There follows that remarkable theatrical moment in which Professor enters and confronts the role-play in mid-flow, the Acting Pseudo-Professor brought face to face with the substantive one: a moment that opens up like a vortex the question of what is what and what is not and, in particular, the high level of indeterminacy in Professor's character. And when Professor first speaks, what registers first and foremost is the lexical cluster on which his utterance is built: 'mystery', 'hidden', 'secret' (8). As the dialogue now proceeds, it is unclear whether Professor is genuinely distracted — unable to recognise that he is facing Samson and Salubi, who are both well known to him — or whether it is a feint (and if it is a feint, to what purpose?). What is foregrounded is Professor's inaccessibility and Samson and Salubi's extreme timidity before him (even in his apparently distracted state, he intimidates them).

While the *mise-en-scène* builds, the stage presence filling with characters in various positions of alliance, detachment and antagonism, Samson signals to Kotonu to distract Professor, and Kotonu offers 'If you like Professor, I will come home with you' (10).[2] In the context of the group stratagem — in the interests of distracting Professor from the role-play he has interrupted — this line need not be read as implying a sexual invitation. What intrigues me, however, is the opportunity it opens up for a reading of Professor as queer and, in particular, the way that in production this might enhance — give an acute edge to — the impact of the power-play Professor engages in with the other characters and of their responses to him. In the context of such a reading, Kotonu's offer would be taken to imply recognition on his part of Professor's desire for him.

Imagine Kotonu delivering that line to suggest the possibility of a sexual invitation. Delivery of this line and of Kotonu's subsequent lines in this interchange would need to establish the production's reading of Kotonu's intention, that is, whether there might be any substance, any underlying hidden erotic agenda behind his invitation, or whether this is purely strategic. This then opens up a new dimension to the

dynamics of propulsion, attraction and repulsion that run throughout the remainder of the play, taking immediate effect with the stand-off that develops out of Kotonu's (Samson-prompted) offer to Professor. Following Professor's response to Kotonu, 'Come then' — and one can imagine the indeterminate intonation and *gestus* with which that line could be delivered — while Kotonu continues to urge, 'Professor, let's go', 'Let's go Professor', Samson, now sensing danger in Kotonu's offer, performs a *volte-face* and tries to hold Kotonu back. Meanwhile, with his more limited perceptiveness, Salubi eggs Kotonu on, solely concerned that Professor should not discover his own culpability in the role-play (11–12). This is a complex stand-off, potentially charged with the articulation, or semi-articulation, of desire, complaisance, self-interest and solicitousness, all within the matrix of the power-play that Professor has engineered. Even after Kotonu has gone off with Professor, the sense of threat and seduction is sustained. Samson bewails the fact that Professor is to show Kotonu the wreckage from another road accident, thus setting back Kotonu's chances of recovering his will to drive: 'This is all Professor's doing' (14). The question arises, what might prompt Professor to act in this way, other than the impulse of sadism, and might that impulse be generated by unarticulated desire for Kotonu?

There is little, if any, material in the text that would disallow a reading of the power-play engaged in by Professor as being intrinsically homoerotic. Again and again, interchanges between Professor and the other characters enable this, witness, *inter alia*:

- Professor's — in the context, outrageous — challenge to Kotonu: 'I have nothing to hide. Have you?' (60);
- The episode in which Samson and Professor discuss Kotonu's crisis of confidence — Samson: 'how can a man cut off part of himself like that. Just look at him. He is not complete without a motor-lorry' (37) — while Kotonu pretends to be asleep, inert, to be haggled over. How deep a degree of disingenuousness might be read into Professor's comment 'What sort of animal is he?'?;
- In respect of the dynamics of attraction and repulsion — Professor reaching out, then retracting with an almost pathological vehemence — the episode in which Professor requests the motor-park inhabitants to sing his favourite praise-song, during which he '*gives short, cynical laughs*', installing himself in queenly fashion as the centre of attention and then dismissing the singers, '*vicious contempt in his voice*' (86–7);
- The cluster of mixed signals — frank recognition of virtue in Samson, derision, challenge — embedded in Professor's comment 'Samson, Lion-hearted Samson with an ass's head, can you not see that your friend [Kotonu] will never drive again?' capped when Samson does not respond as hoped with Professor's first, and threatening, acknowledgment that he has recognised Samson earlier, caricaturing him in the role-play (47);

- After a long interchange with Samson, as if sympathetic engagement is too painful, too self-revealing, Professor's comment 'Get out of my sight', the sadism inherent in this marked in Samson's response, '[*almost tearfully*] But you must help me' (Soyinka 50).

This repeated oscillation between acts of invitation and repulsion climaxes, of course, in the murder of Professor, an event that he calls upon himself. Standard readings of the meaning of this denouement include the recognition of Professor's blasphemy, his expropriation of the masquerade in the interests of his own quest to pin down the meaning of the life/death continuum, and the mixed motivations of Salubi and Say Tokyo Kid, who carry out the killing. These interpretations hold. In addition, one needs to note how graphically Soyinka's stage direction describes the murder and the phallic thrust of the knife-blow that kills Professor:

*Suddenly [Professor and Say Tokyo Kid] lock. With no sound but hissed breaths they heave and gripe [sic] at each other in a tense elastic control ... Say Tokyo ... plunges the knife in Professor's back. Professor jerks upright, his face masked in pain.* (97)

But Biodun Jeyifo's account of the episode in Yvonne Brewster's 1992 production suggests how the meaning of the event can be opened out further as, after Professor's death, 'all the other characters in the play descended on Professor's dead body and stripped it of every salvageable item of clothing' (Jeyifo, 'Whose Theatre' 461). Jeyifo sees in this – rightly, I think – an act of 'cannibalization', a 'brilliantly original extemporization by Brewster' that clarifies the play's concern with 'the predatoriness of capitalist commodity fetishism' (Jeyifo, 'Whose Theatre' 461).[3] But the stage picture Jeyifo describes, specifically in respect of his use of the term 'cannibalization', is consonant, too, with a reading of Professor as gay predator *manqué* and of his end: it resonates uncannily with the fate of Sebastian, the closet homosexual in Tennessee Williams's *Suddenly, Last Summer*, who is stripped and then devoured by the youths on whom he has been preying.

*The Road* is, as with so much of Soyinka's work, about power and the playing out of power relations. Here, Soyinka explores power relations in their intersecting vertical and horizontal formations: vertical, in respect of the tight net of relationships that obtains between the inhabitants of the motor-park; horizontal, in respect of the wider context, which includes the social economy Jeyifo alludes to in his essay 'The Hidden Class War' and the political crisis enveloping the South and Mid-West of Nigeria at the time of the play's writing. While most of the references Professor makes to his instrumentality within the wider context are disingenuous, his role within the vertical set of power relations is clearly crucial. This holds, even though at one point he insists, 'I make no one do anything' (61), a comment that may be strictly true, to the extent that it could be claimed by Lady Macbeth or the

Witches, but which is untrue to the same degree. In production, a reading of Professor as queer might add a cogent and troubling dimension to the play's exploration of power relations, without reducing the complex web of meanings that any production of *The Road* must convey.

## Notes

1  In the body of the text Soyinka indicates that the masquerade referred to and also enacted (twice) in the play is *egungun*, widespread throughout the South-West (predominantly Yoruba) region of Nigeria, while the *agemo* cult and its ritual performances are specifically rooted in religious practice in the town of Ijebu-Ode. I have not seen any discussion of this apparent discrepancy (or open-endedness) – Soyinka's use of *agemo* in the prefatory poem and of *egungun* in the stage directions – but this is something that might be worth looking into. Though a common source for the two has been argued, *agemo* cannot simply be regarded as a variant of *egungun*. Unlike *egungun*, for example, *agemo* can hardly be regarded as an ancestor cult. This is a highly complex and difficult topic: two comments by Margaret Thompson Drewal seem to me, however, germane to the underlying presence of *agemo* in *The Road*: that 'the more chaos and noise, the more the ethos of Agemo is felt' (Drewal 114–15) and that 'conflict is endemic in Agemo performance' (125).
2  In the context of the present reading of this episode, it is worth noting that Professor acknowledges that he recognises Kotonu — 'I do know *you*. You are the coast-to-coast driver who gave up the road' (10). There is no simple explanation for his singling out Kotonu, who is as, but no more, familiar to him than Samson or Salubi.
3  For 'extemporization' here read 'strong reading'. Jeyifo's comments extend from his groundbreaking essay 'The Hidden Class War in *The Road*'. Another feature of the Brewster production that Jeyifo records – disapprovingly – is the 'strong element of camp' with which the closing *egungun* was staged (Jeyifo, 'Whose Theatre' 460). Not having seen the production I cannot comment on this, but in respect of the kind of queer reading of Professor's role that I am suggesting, a more conventional emphasis on the hyper-masculinity of *egungun* might be appropriate.

## Works Cited

Drewal, Margaret Thompson. *Yoruba Ritual: Performers, Play, Agency.* Bloomington: Indiana UP, 1992.
Dunton, Chris. 'Back on *The Road* again: Soyinka's Professor and *Vodou*'s Baron Samedi'. *Yoruba Creativity.* Eds. Toyin Falola and Ann Genova. Trenton, NJ and Asmara: Africa World Press, 2005.
Eagleton, Terry. *Criticism and Ideology.* London: New Left Books, 1976.
Fatoba, Femi. 'Developing a Theatre Role'. *Glendora Review* 1.3 (1996): 66–68.
Gikandi, Simon. *Wole Soyinka's The Road.* Nairobi: Heinemann, 1985.

Hoad, Neville. 'Decolonizing the Body: Race, Homosexuality, Africa and African. America in Wole Soyinka's *The Interpreters*'. *African Intimacies: Race, Homosexuality and Globalization in African Literature and History*. Neville Hoad. Minneapolis: U of Minnesota P, 2006.

Jeyifo, Biodun. 'The Hidden Class War in *The Road*'. *The Truthful Lie: Essays in a Sociology of African Drama*. Biodun Jeyifo. London: New Beacon Books, 1985.

———. 'Whose Theatre, Whose Africa? Wole Soyinka's *The Road* on the Road'. *Modern Drama* XLV (2002): 449–65.

Katrak, Ketu. *Wole Soyinka and Modern Tragedy: A Study of Dramatic Theory and Practice*. Westport, Conn.: Greenwood Press, 1986.

Lindfors, Bernth. 'African Directors Abroad'. *Theatron* 3.1/2 (2005): 19–29.

Mike, Chuck. *Soyinka as Director: Interview with Chuck Mike*. Ife: Department of English, U of Ife, 1986.

Soyinka, Wole. *The Road*. Oxford: Oxford UP, 1965.

Wright, Derek. *Wole Soyinka Revisited*. New York: Twayne, 1993.

© Michael Dauda

# d'bi young

## revolushun III

i'm screaming revolushun in the name of the people
until i stop to ask my people
what does it take to make a revolushun
is there space for hate in a revolushun
can i be consumed by hate and make a revolushun

*sisters and brothers we need to unite (raised fist)*
*but i hate those fucking homo bastards (hitler salute)*
*brothers and sisters we need to stand up and fight*
  *(raised fist)*
*but i hate those lesbian bitches (hitler salute)*
*sisters and brothers we need to speak the right*
  *(raised fist)*
*all those queer and transvestites fire bun dem (hitler*
  *salute)*

is there space for hate in a revolushun
can i be consumed by hate and make a revolushun

*hot damn*
*when i catch me a nigger*
*i like to string him by his little nigger neck*
*you know how dem niggers be hollering*
*but den you hear that pop*
*when the nigger neck snaps*
*den that fat nigger tongue comes hanging out*
*i like to see that nigger tongue hanging*
*and those big fucking nigger eyes*
*popping out all scared*
*i love to see me a scared nigger*
*dat's how you know*

*you done got another one a*
*dem nigger bastards*
*we done got another slave nigger bastards*

from days not so old
they sold and hung our souls

centuries fair barter
erased
new economic structure
racialization of skin colour
demonization of afrikan culture
slaughter
my people
do we remember

those days of old
they sold and hung our souls

now we are
hunting
beating
beseeching
begging
and yearning
for the hanging
the lynching
the murdering
the fire burning
of a sistren
or brethren
thirsty for blood
blood sucking
filled with hate
hate preaching

*Wasafiri Vol. 22, No. 1 March 2007, pp. 66–68*
ISSN 0269-0055 print/ISSN 1747-1508 online © 2007 d'bi young
http://www.tandf.co.uk/journals    DOI: 10.1080/02690050601097740

do we remember

we been through persecution
and now we persecute
missa youth what-a-gwaan
come quick and gimme likkle truth
mi nuh know how fi understand di shituashun
everyday wi get up and preach revolushun
to di nation
how mi fi hate mi breddah man because him love
    anoddah man
how mi fi hate mi sistah gyal because she love
    anoddah gyal
so mi fi hate myself cause mi love oomaan and man
mi fi hate myself cause mi love man an oomaan
wi been through persecution and now wi persecute
missa youth what-a-gwaan
come quick and gimme likkle truth

did we work for the right
to perpetuate hate
our slave daddies
taught us well
how to hate

*(hitler salute)*
*hatehatehatehatehatehatehate*
*i hate those fucking homo bastards*
*hatehatehatehatehatehatehate*
*i hate those fucking nigger bitches*
*hatehatehatehatehatehatehate*
*i hate those queer motherfuckers*
*fire bun dem to all black niggers*
*fucking slaves*
*judgement for all batty man and sodomite*
*you're going straight to hell*
*hatehatehatehatehatehatehate*
*i hate you and you you and you and you and you*
*and you know what if i was white i would fucking hate*
    *black people too*
*as a matter of fact i do*
*all you fucking dyke*
*queer*
*gay motherfuckers*

what does it take to make a revolushun
is there space for hate in a revolushun

i cannot scream revolushun in the name
    of the people
until i stop to ask my people
can i be consumed by hate and make a revolushun

there is no room for hate in my revolushun

## letter to tchaiko

tchaiko negotiating this hybridism is a challenge. I have no place to place these contrived memories of mine. I did not experience that side of jamaica. but I know it exists. womben who are amazons having to reinvent themselves. like the snake. the goddess. so they can stay on top of the game. as opposed to underneath it. as dis shitstem would have it. we need to return and tell of the truths. weaved into lies. then sold to us.

I was born and raised in maxfield avenue kingston 13. never left till I was 15. so it's kindah fresh in my mind. but not fresh enough. I remember walking barefooted. cuz I loved the feel of concrete jungle. I knew even then that that shit was making me tough. like I would need to be. whether I stayed in jamaica or not. I remember fighting through my working class status at campion college. the first half of which I spent twisting my tongue into the queens english. the latter half I spent showing off my 'patois' because I was *authentic ghetto*. moved to canada and got some legitimization for my outspoken wombanism. didn't need to shake the habit of liking the ways womben's breath felt under my breasts.

moving from jamaica liberated and stifled me in so many ways. I moved to toronto in 1993 and you know how that shit goes. first lost. then found. then you hang out somewhere in between. a hybrid. dub poetry is my link. had it taught to me in that old griot-tradishun way. by my mother. anita stewart. now here I am, trying to reclaim the wombanism in the art. so I rhyme about bleeding. and androgyny. and di maroons. and womben's rituals. and struggle. and death. and liberation. and love. I rhyme about love. I came to cuba a year ago on a family myth that my grandfather was cuban. and also needing to be in jamaica but not knowing how. I came to cuba instead. with a freshly shaved head. a huge smile. a loud mouth. but no words to speak spanish. oh and I came with a little money. had the idea to create music here. the language barrier worked for me. playing with an all male band singing BLOOD.

singing that to an all male band. it helps if the band only has an *idea* of what you are talking about. the language barrier gave me enough time to earn people's love and trust. time for them to release their defences to this womban defending life. I left 5 months later with a demo cd. on the promise that I would return and pay people properly for a full length professional album. two weeks before I left. I fell in love. with hakema. I mean what do I know about that love business . . . but fi real. all the tentative energy around this kindah of love. all the economic fucked-up-ness of being foreigner and friend. my favourite thing to say to people here was/is 'i am jamaican. i was born and raised in di ghetto. trust me i know.' that does not account for the fact that i am also canadian. a canadian government recognized and supported artist. i go and come as i please. i have a home in canada. i no longer occupy the same economic class/space I did when I was growing up in maxfield avenue. what a flip of di script. each time i come to cuba i am faced with this reality. in canada i am a queer working class artist. who lives on the margins by choice. when i come here. i am north american. who doesn't speak very good spanish and who flies like i am taking a walk down the street. the average cuban does not have that kind of access to air travel. always negotiating this hybridism and knowing that the choices i make around who i love and how i love them are always political cuz everything is political.

*Wasafiri* no 51 Summer 2007

Clare Short

Robert Eaglestone

Adhaf Soueif

Pankaj Mishra

Tsitsi Dangarembga

Ishtyak Shukri

Everlyn Nicodemus

Writing through Terror

# Luke Reid

*Sycorax*

Swollen,
with my eyes bleared blue round their pockets,
they let me live and shipped me off with sailors
as the fogbound shores of my home, Algiers,
slipped out like the two strands of a ribbon.

We came to outer shores then, and the captain
motioned up for a flit-noted tucket.
I cackled in the cracked faces of my jailors,
their standing-to, their ceremony for an old hag
    sorcerer.
They were spooked though; not even the boatswain

would touch my rags when they left me on the sand.
Alone, I screeched and shook like the island cicadas
until the child fell from me to my bruised-red feet
in a rush of gop and caul. And with a grey slate
I cut the cord and held the stuttering boy in hand.

Together we found the brine-pits of the island,
the springs and cowslips, the waterlily armadas,
and promised each other we'd never leave.
But I died, as all man must, and now my son is slave
to that witch Prospero: like me, an exiled shaman.

*Wasafiri Vol. 22, No. 1 March 2007, p. 69*
ISSN 0269-0055 print/ISSN 1747-1508 online © 2007 Wasafiri
http://www.tandf.co.uk/journals      DOI: 10.1080/00324720601124334

Routledge
Taylor & Francis Group

# Louise Bennett,
# Voice of a People

*Linton Kwesi Johnson*

Louise Bennett-Coverley, also known as Miss Lou, a legend in her lifetime who earned iconic status in her native Jamaica, died on 26 July 2006 aged eighty-six. Poet, actress, comedienne, broadcaster, folklorist, teacher and social commentator, she is a household name in Jamaica and celebrated abroad. With the exception of Marcus Garvey, I cannot think of any other Jamaican who has had a greater impact on the shaping of the nation's identity. Her influence on Jamaican culture is phenomenal. She has made a significant contribution in helping the Jamaican people come to terms with their African heritage, valorising the culture of the folk.

Her greatest achievement was to rehabilitate, elevate and validate the spoken language of the people, Jamaican Creole, through her poetry. As Mervyn Morris asserts:

> She was a patriot committed to correcting the colonial legacy of self-contempt and she cleared the way for others by demonstrating that Jamaican Creole could be the medium of significant art. (*Guardian*)

She used irony disguised in laughter to offer Jamaican people a mirror in which they could see themselves. Her impact was not limited to Jamaica; she is regarded as the most influential Caribbean writer for bringing Creole 'into the foreground of West Indian cultural life' (Morris, *Guardian*) and is recognised as a poet of international significance.

Louise Simone Bennett, an only child, was born on 7 September 1919 in Kingston, Jamaica. Her mother, Kerene Robinson, was a dressmaker and her father, Augustus Cornelius Bennett, a baker who died when she was seven years old. Her love of Jamaican talk and her talent for performing were nurtured by her mother and grandmother, Mimi. She attended Calabar Elementary School, St Simon's College and Excelsior High School in Kingston and Friend's College in Highgate, St Mary. At school she liked literature and tried her hand at writing verse in English. She wrote her first Jamaican 'dialect' poem, 'On a Tram Car', when she was fourteen years old. The poem was well received by schoolmates so she continued to write more in her native tongue and began performing them at free concerts. In 1938 she received her first professional fee from local impresario Eric 'Chalk Talk' Coverley, who in 1954 became her husband. In 1943 her poems began to appear regularly in the *Jamaican Gleaner*. Her best-known publications are *Jamaica Labrish*

*Wasafiri Vol. 22, No. 1 March 2007, pp. 70–71*
ISSN 0269-0055 print/ISSN 1747-1508 online © 2007 Linton Kwesi Johnson
http://www.tandf.co.uk/journals    DOI: 10.1080/02690050601097773

((1966)), *Anancy and Miss Lou* (1979), *Selected Poems* ((1982)) and *Aunty Roachy Seh* (1993).

Although she had been publishing books since 1942, it was not until 1963 when Mervyn Morris wrote his seminal essay, 'On Reading Louise Bennett Seriously', that Miss Lou began to receive critical attention and acclaim. Other academics who have looked at her work include Gordon Rohlehr, Carolyn Cooper, Lloyd Brown and Rex Nettleford. A decade after Morris's essay, Louise Bennett began receiving numerous awards and honours, including the MBE, the Order of Jamaica and the Order of Merit from the Jamaican government in 2001. Most recently, she became a Fellow of the Institute of Jamaica in 2003.

An accomplished actress and comedienne, Miss Lou brought laughter into the lives of three generations of Jamaicans. She was regarded as the first lady of Jamaican theatre. She made a significant contribution to the Jamaicanisation of the Little Theatre Movement's national pantomime as actress, writer, lyricist and director, and performed in twenty-five productions between 1943 and 1975. A British Council scholarship allowed her to hone her theatrical talent at the Royal Academy for the Dramatic Arts (RADA) in Britain from 1945 to 1947, and she performed with repertory companies in Amersham, Coventry and Huddersfield. After a brief sojourn in the USA between 1953 and 1955, during which she worked in radio, sang folk songs and married Eric Coverley, they returned to Jamaica where they resided for the next three decades. In the early 1980s they migrated to the USA and eventually settled in Canada.

It was largely through radio and later, television, that Miss Lou became a household name in Jamaica. Her broadcasting career began when she was a student at RADA and was given her own programme by the BBC. After graduating in 1947 she went back to Jamaica and returned to England in 1950 to work on the BBC radio programme, *West Indian Guest Night*. Jamaicans will remember her local radio shows *Laugh with Louise*, the *Aunty Roachy Seh* series and *The Lou and Ranny Show*. Her television show *Ring Ding* captivated and delighted children during the 1970s.

Louise Bennett was a scholar of Jamaica's folklore and oral culture which she had begun to study whilst a student at Friend's College and continued during the 1950s when she worked as Drama Officer for the Jamaica Social Welfare Commission, travelling all over the island. She was consulted by lexicographers and scholars and lectured on drama and folklore for the Extramural department of the University of the West Indies.

It was in her capacity as a scholar that I first met Miss Lou in 1981 when I was doing research for my BBC radio series, *From Mento to Lovers Rock*, on the history of modern popular Jamaican music. Miss Lou was very accommodating, warm, charming and hospitable. The information I got from her was invaluable in putting the series together. Then in 1983, I couldn't believe my luck when Miss Lou invited me to do a couple of items with her on stage during a rare performance in London at the Lyric Theatre in Hammersmith. Together we performed the folk song 'Under the Coconut Tree' and the word game 'Mawnin Buddy'. The show was recorded and released as the album *Yes M'Dear – Miss Lou Live* by Island Records. Some of Miss Lou's other recordings include *Jamaica Singing Games* (1953), *Listen to Louise* (1968) and *The Honourable Miss Lou* (1981).

Several Caribbean artists, including the Jamaican dub poets, have acknowledged the enormous debt owed to Louise Bennett. In Britain we have our own Miss Lou in the poet Valerie Bloom. Mervyn (Morris) tells us in his essay, 'Miss Lou, Some Heirs and Successors', that:

> Joan Andrea Hutchinson and Amina Blackwood Meeks, distinctly talented writers and precisely effective performers, have absorbed and, in their differing ways, have begun to extend the creative legacy of Louise Bennett. (82)

Louise Bennett was given the official funeral that her creative accomplishments, her life's work, merited, and buried at National Heroes Park in Kingston, Jamaica, with her husband. I am sure I am not the only Jamaican who hopes that it will be just a matter of time before Miss Lou joins Nanny of the Maroons to become Jamaica's second national heroine.

## Works Cited and Select Bibliography

Bennett, Louise. *Jamaica Labrish*. Kingston, Jamaica: Sangster's Book Stores, 1966.

——. *Selected Poems*. Ed. Mervyn Morris. Kingston, Jamaica: Sangster's Book Stores, 1982.

——. *Yes M'Dear – Miss Lou Live*. (Recording). London: Island Records, 1983.

Morris, Mervyn. 'Miss Lou, Some Heirs and Successors'. *Making West Indian Literature*. Kingston and Miami: Ian Randle Publishers, 2005. 75–83.

——. 'Obituary: Louise Bennett-Coverley'. *Guardian* 1 Aug 2006: 32.

# Reviews

Denise deCaires Narain

## Stories of Women: Gender and Narrative in the Postcolonial Nation

Elleke Boehmer

*Manchester University Press,*
*Manchester and New York, 2005, hb*
239pp ISBN 0 7190 6878 9
www.manchesteruniversitypress.co.uk

This collection of essays offers discussions of an impressively wide range of literary texts from diverse postcolonial contexts and in relation to an engaging gamut of postcolonial concerns and theoretical approaches. The intersecting vectors of nation and gender tie the essays loosely together and make this a welcome addition to the growing body of work which consolidates the importance of gender in postcolonial studies. It also challenges the current antipathy to 'the nation' within postcolonial studies, arguing that it may yet provide an accommodating space for women and for women's access to modernity.

*Stories of Women* argues from the outset that nation inevitably bears the imprint of gender:

As in the cross-section of a tree trunk that is nowhere unmarked by its grain — by that pattern expressing its history — so, too, is nation informed throughout by its gendered history, by the normative masculinities and femininities that have shaped its growth over time.

Each of the essays then traces the 'markings' of gender in a selection of literary texts, largely (though not exclusively) by South Asian and African writers, male and female. Chapter One, 'Theorising the engendered nation', makes the now familiar argument that in many male-authored texts, 'woman' functions as metaphor while 'man' functions as agent in the struggle for nationhood. Whether it is in the celebration of Mother Africa or Mother India, Boehmer argues that images of women are deployed as crucial symbols of *both* the ideal *and* failed/diseased (post-independence) nation. Familial relationships are also important, structuring the representation of nation, either by implication in the earnest stories of questing 'sons of the (African) soil' in texts by Laye and Abrahams or, more ironically, in the elaborate use made of family trees and national genealogies by Rushdie. In what she calls, following Freud, the *family drama*, Boehmer suggests that the family is both a constitutive of, and privileged paradigm for, the nation. In the one

chapter which does not focus on postcolonial *novels*, 'The hero's story: the male leader's autobiography and the syntax of postcolonial nationalism', Boehmer argues persuasively that postcolonial male leaders narrate their stories in ways which naturalise this familial paradigm of the nation, and of their roles as sons within it. The comparative reading of Mandela's *Long Walk to Freedom* (1994) and Nehru's *An Autobiography* (1936) is sharp and the astute connections made with a range of autobiographical texts and theories of autobiography makes this a meaty essay.

Chapters Two and Three focus on two prominent 'fathers' of African Literature, Achebe and Ngugi who both attempt to inscribe women as powerful forces in their texts but fail because these figures are so overloaded with (good) symbolic value that they become 'bionic' superwomen, and unbelievable. Boehmer recognises the effort involved for both writers but concludes that the old 'gender markings' creep in to compromise their good intentions. By contrast, Flora Nwapa, whose novel *Efuru* (1966) was the first to be published by an Anglophone African woman, offers a take on the nation which, because it is embedded in the daily rituals of a specific community *within* the nation and inscribes this polyvocal reality in the *form* of the novel

*Wasafiri Vol. 22, No. 1 March 2007, pp. 72–88*
ISSN 0269-0055 print/ISSN 1747-1508 online © 2007 Wasafiri
http://www.tandf.co.uk/journals    DOI: 10.1080/02690050601097864

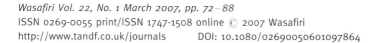

Routledge
Taylor & Francis Group

itself, refuses male-authored grand narratives of the nation. It is hard to disagree with this, but the very inevitability of this argument perhaps raises questions about an approach which hinges on women's writing coming *after* male-authored texts and then functioning as a *corrective* account. In a literal sense, many African women's texts have *come after* those of their male counterparts; as Boehmer points out, Flora Nwapa has been referred to as one of 'the sons of Achebe'. But, as feminist critics, we are also now writing *after* the various critical interventions that have so thoroughly destabilised taken-for-granted categories, including 'woman'. This makes the business of tracking gendered representations in texts in tandem with the author's own sexed identity an altogether trickier affair.

Chapter Six, 'Daughters of the house: the adolescent girl and the nation' shifts away from interrogating male-authored texts to offer comparative readings of women's texts published between 1883 and 2002 from diverse postcolonial locations. Instead of a (rather dreary) catalogue of where/how male writers get the representation of woman wrong, this chapter looks at three women's texts in the context of Schreiner's novel, *The Story of an African Farm* (1883) and offers a dynamic discussion of the way that daughters, of

the (patriarchal) family *and* nation, negotiate a place for themselves. The choice of texts is unexpected: Christina Stead's *The Man Who Loved Children* (1940), Buchi Emecheta's *Destination Biafra* (1982) and Carol Shields' *Unless* (2002) but Boehmer really makes the comparison work, offering subtle and nuanced arguments about the ways each 'daughter' authors a sense of 'self', however compromised. None of the (re)solutions suggested in the texts is completely convincing but harnessing them together, she argues, does present possibilities for women's agency within family *and* nation. This commitment to a comparative, relational approach is persuasive and is extended in most of the remaining chapters to good effect.

Chapter Seven explores the way the traumatised colonial body is embodied or avoided in novels by Head, Coetzee, Farah, Okri and Cliff while Chapter Eight discusses the very different attitudes to metaphorising the nation in novels by Okri, Hove and Marachera. Gender slips out of focus a little in the latter chapter and the assertion with which it opens that 'anti-colonial nationalism in Africa, as in other colonised regions, was distinguished by *literal* belief structures: a strong, teleological faith in the actual existence of the nation as "people"' perhaps takes anti-colonial elites too much at their word. The marginalisation of 'First Nation' peoples in definitions of the postcolonial nation was too categorical for it to be read as innocent of racially stratifying arguments from the outset.

The last four essays focus exclusively on texts by women consolidating the value of comparative readings in a 'transnational frame'. Chapters Eleven and Twelve anchor the arguments more firmly in relation to gender and nation; in the former Boehmer argues that Yvonne Vera and Arundhati Roy share a similar concern with the *local* spaces which women occupy, offering in their texts 'more heterogeneous constructions of community' which ultimately suggest more complex and accommodating definitions of nation. Cross-cultural

comparative readings can thus ironically end up consolidating the specificity of the local; a persuasive point. In Chapter Twelve, Boehmer argues that the 'small stories' of rebellion, domestic duties, pleasures and desires explored in Manju Kapur's novels about (middle class) Indian women refuse the definition of nation as normatively male, suggesting instead that 'the (re-) gendered nation might be reclaimed as a structure of feeling, if not of passion, for women'.

*Stories of Women* offers *excellent* discussions of a wonderfully eclectic range of literary texts in pleasingly unexpected combinations. The collection as a whole both enacts and endorses the productive possibilities of the collaborative, the comparative, the speculative and the relational: all of which are a welcome relief from the grandstanding combativeness of some postcolonial debate. If at times assertions of the ongoing viability of 'the nation' appear to be an act of faith in the absence of any other clearly definable alternative, this may perhaps be reasonably viewed as a predicament of our postcolonial moment?

I'll end with a couple of quibbles: the first concerns the 'neo-orientalist' reception of Roy's *The God of Small Things* (1997). Using a similar line of argument to Graham Huggan in *The Postcolonial Exotic* (2001), Boehmer suggests that the ecstatic reception of Roy's novel frequently referenced Roy's 'Indianness', her exotic 'intensely feminine, ineffably photogenic, elfin beauty' and the fashionably hybrid exuberance of her writing style. To avoid such neo-orientalising processes, Boehmer suggests that postcolonial critics attend to the material realities and specific contexts informing such expressions of hybridity and refuse to privilege only those texts which enact hybridity. Although Boehmer mentions kathakali dance, it strikes me that the discussion requires (as did Huggan's) a full discussion of the considerable amount of coverage given to the reception of Roy's text *in India* for this argument to begin to persuade. If arguments about 'the postcolonial exotic' remain tied exclusively to *metropolitan* consumption, don't we risk a pervasive cynicism which denies the possibility of ethical readings of any 'hybrid' postcolonial text?

I wonder too about the argument made in Chapter Ten about the taboo on same-sex relationships in Africa and in African literature and that 'sexuality remains the dark secret of the Third World nation'. This perhaps overstates the case and ignores the many novels in which sexuality is central to the narrative (and to ideas of nation); Armah's hypermasculine protagonists and the violent homophobia of *Two Thousand Seasons* would be one example from the 1960s but, more recently, to take just one postcolonial context, same-sex relationships have featured more prominently in several South African texts (including Shamim Sarif's *The World Unseen*, Achmat Dangor's *Bitter Fruit*, Gordimer's *None to Accompany Me* and Coetzee's *Disgrace*). Boehmer offers a queer reading of close relationships between women in Vera and Dangarembga as indicative of 'yearning and desire' even where there is no explicit sexual relationship. The embrace of queerness may provide a 'restorative aesthetics' and a move towards 'an epistemology of African queerness' to counter the 'overcompensatory mechanism of a defensive African masculinity'. While I agree with the gist of the argument and with the expansiveness of this gesture, it strikes me that explicitly naming it 'queer' in combative relationship to a 'defensive African masculinity' may be provocative but not productive and risks re-inscribing the 'dominant' position being challenged in the first place. I don't have an alternative to offer to Boehmer's 'postcolonial aesthetics of queerness' but the arguments she presents in *Stories of Women* offer detailed literary mappings of the intersections of 'gender' and 'nation' which will undoubtedly influence the contours of postcolonial feminism — and help generate a more nuanced vocabulary.

## Kanika Batra

### Because I Have a Voice: Queer Politics in India

#### Arvind Narrain and Gautam Bhan, eds

*Yoda Press, New Delhi, 2005, pb*
ISBN 8 1902 2722 X INR 295
www.yodapress.com

People Tree, my favourite haunt in Connaught Place, New Delhi, keeps a selection of very special literature in a small bookstore at the back of the shop. This is the place where I first discovered a collection of books documenting the lives and struggles of sexual minorities in India. It is easy to miss the shelf containing these books and indeed the bookstore unless one knows where to look for it, as much as it is easy to miss the presence of gay, lesbian, and bisexual men and women amongst the multiple social spaces inhabited by most Indians. Except that these lives are no longer invisible. They are here, many of them are out and some, though not all, proudly announce that they are queer. Assisting in this endeavour is Yoda Press, a progressive publishing house whose recent title includes a collection of essays edited by Arvind Narrain and Gautam Bhan entitled *Because I Have a Voice,* documenting the rise of queer politics in India.

Besides several activist publications on gay and lesbian rights in India, Ashwini Sukthankar and Hoshang Merchant's anthologies of lesbian and gay writing, Ruth Vanita and Saleem Kidwai's anthology on same-sex love, and Vanita's edited collection on queer readings of Indian culture and society are some of the precursors of *Because I Have a Voice*. Narrain and Bhan's introduction to the volume testifies that the sexuality awareness work of the 1980s, which reached its apogee in the late 1990s, following the controversy surrounding the screening of Deepa Mehta's 'lesbian' film *Fire* in Indian cinemas, has now come to be theorised

as a fully-fledged political movement. Including theoretical accounts, activist reports, and life narratives of people living on the boundaries of acceptable and transgressive modes of expressing gender and sexual identity, the essays in this volume mark the emergence of 'a more public queer articulation'. In the opinion of many contributors to the volume 'queerness' does not imply merely an alternative sexual preference (gay or lesbian) or a crossover to a non-biologically assigned gender identity but rather an interrogation of the patriarchal and heterosexist premises governing Indian social spaces (Bhan and Narrain, Narrain and Chandran, Muraleedharan).

One of the signs of the increasing sophistication of queer politics in India is that the movement is able to critique itself by building on the work done over the past few years. Discussing legal, medical, and cinematic discourses, the first section of the anthology attempts to provide a conceptual approach to sexuality as a form of politics. Akshay Khanna's essay in this section takes issue with the two most common ways of addressing the politics of sexuality: as a human rights issue and as a response to violence. Pointing to the pitfalls of both approaches Khanna indicates how the postcolonial state becomes an arbiter of a sexual politics since the 'human rights regime is located in the relationship between the body and the state' and 'for the working of power to be recognised and addressed, it must be manifested as violence, or it should be capable of being understood in terms of "discrimination"'.

These insights are relevant both to a queer as well as a feminist politics, addressed by many activist reports included in the volume. Among others Chayanika Shah, Gomathi N B, Bina Fernandez, and Deepa V N bring the issue of the highs and lows of a collaborative feminist and queer activism to the forefront in the second section of the volume entitled 'Stories of Struggle'. While Indian feminists have been reluctant to ally with groups focusing on sexuality rights, sexuality framed through a focus on violence against women has always been on the agenda of the feminist framework. As Deepa points out in her meticulously documented report of the origins, activities, and future of the organisation Sahayatrika (literally, fellow traveller), such a focus in the prevailing feminist practice 'leaves unaddressed perhaps more challenging and disruptive notions of sexual and personal as well as socio-economic autonomy'. The challenge is to 'move beyond presenting a lesbian existence as a site of violence and conceive of a lesbian (or feminist) politics that is based on the right to desire'. The women's movement is the natural ally of the queer movement in this respect, since, according to Chayanika, 'women's movements were the first to articulate concern over the control over sexuality and the societal constructions of gender and are hence the closest link and support for the nascent "queer" movements in the country'. Bina and Gomathi's research on violence faced by lesbian women in India situates itself in a feminist standpoint epistemology marked by an assertion of their identities as bisexual and lesbian activists. Locating several sites of institutional violence, among them the family and the medical establishment, the implications of this research help theorise violence in a nuanced manner by not only documenting the possible causes of the high incidence of lesbian suicides in India but also accounting for the violence implicit in disallowing sex reassignment surgery to those who desire it.

Sex reassignment surgery to adopt a transsexual identity is a vexed and contentious issue in queer communities. Even while pointing to the violence implicit in the denial of rights to transsexuals Fernandez and Gomathi label lesbians' desire for such surgery as indicative of 'some degree of self-denial and violence towards their bodies'. Indeed the one article on the rights of transsexuals included in the volume expresses unease with the idea: Ashwini

Sukthankar admits that her initial opinion was that such surgery 'reified the rigid definitions of gender – what it means to be a man or a woman – that feminists had always sought to question'. By including two accounts – the first by Satya, a female to male transsexual, and the second by Famila, a hijra – in the essay Sukthankar makes an important intervention in the conjunctures and disjunctures between the two identities. Members of a community indigenous to South Asia, hijras are men who willingly embrace a female identity following voluntary (though sometimes enforced) castration. They earn their living as performers on auspicious occasions such as weddings or the birth of children in families. The historical, class-specific, and linguistic differences between hijras and transsexuals helps in accounting for the different forms of queer existence indigenous to South Asian, particularly Indian, contexts.

These identities also counter the charge of Westernisation faced by the queer movement in India and other non-Western locations. The class specific dimensions of this charge are evinced in Alok Gupta's account titled 'Englishpur ki Kothi' ('The Kothi from Englishland') where another identity specific to Indian context, kothi (feminised men in same sex relationships, often as passive partners) is applied to the author but his English education and class position are seen as setting him off from other kothis. The central problematic here is the lack of applicability of Western identity categories to many forms of alternative relationships found in India — between women, men or transsexuals.

This volume provides nuanced information on queer lives in India. It is also a veritable archive of queer activist support networks: Humsafar, Humrahi and Humnawaz from New Delhi, Sahayatrika from Kerala, Lesbians and Bisexuals in Action (LABIA) from Bombay, Counsel Club and Parivartak from Calcutta, Amitie from Chandanagar, Good as You (GAY) from Bangalore, among others. For young people embarking on the search for their sexual

identities, this archive of organisational work and life narratives is as important as is the reiteration of the importance of queer visibility in university campuses. Representation in its broadest sense is clearly intended by the editors since there are accounts of Christian, Muslim and Hindu sexual identities based in India and as well as queer communities in the Indian diaspora. Meticulously edited, for the most part free from typographical errors, this book does its share in providing visibility to queer lives and the queer political movement in India where the relative merits of such visibility continue to be debated within the movement.

## Andrew Lesk

### Swimming in the Monsoon Sea

Shyam Selvadurai

Tundra Books, Toronto, 2005, hb
274pp ISBN 0 8877 6735 4 $24.99 Cdn
www.tundrabooks.com

### Story-Wallah: Short Fiction from South Asian Writers

Syham Selvadurai, ed.

Houghton Mifflin, New York, 2005, pb
438pp ISBN 0 6185 7680 0 $14.00 US
www.marinerbooks.com

In his new novel, ostensibly for young adults, Shyam Selvadurai mines territory familiar to those who have read his 1994 effort, *Funny Boy*. *Swimming in the Monsoon Sea*, like its predecessor, concerns a young boy's growing realisation of his nascent homosexuality. *Funny Boy*, though, engages the panorama of Sri Lanka's social strife and search for national identity as a parallel backdrop to the protagonist's search for personal identity; the new work, on the other hand, uses a much smaller palate to examine how a sexual coming-of-age is difficult in a country not known for a liberal attitude toward identities queer.

Amrith de Alwis is a fourteen-year-old orphan, living with his well-to-do relatives in Colombo, in 1980. A sensitive youth, Amrith is a relative loner with no male friends, and an adolescent's penchant for holding onto a peevish anger. His Aunty Bundle blames herself for the death of Amrith's mother, and though we later learn that her guilt is misplaced, Amrith nevertheless uses it as a bargaining chip in maintaining his hard-done-by stance.

The novel opens with Amrith's attempt to make a silent mynah bird speak, and it is the bird's unwillingness to accommodate itself to another's wishes that is meant to parallel Amrith's reluctance to disclose his feelings to those who might help him, notably his aunt. Similarly, the turbulence of the monsoon sea, appearing occasionally, is a pathetic fallacy signaling Amrith's own disordered uncertainties and lack of self-knowledge.

The attentive reader, though, will easily intuit what Amrith cannot: his increasingly obvious homosexuality. Rather stereotypically, Amrith is a star of his school's drama society and relishes playing the female roles in his school's various productions of Shakespeare. He has won an award for his portrayal of Juliet and is now eager to play Desdemona. His drama teacher, Madam Algama, 'had a way of looking at him, as if she saw right into his soul and understood something about him that he did not understand about himself. And what she saw made her more kind to him, more gentle'. He finds great contentment in the aesthetic luster of his Aunt Wilhelmina's silver, which he polishes. And he has befriended his Aunty Bundle's friend, the very gay Lucien Lindamulagé, who we find, in a chapter appropriately named 'The Holidays Drag On', 'always applied white powder to his face'. With Lucien, 'Amrith felt that he could simply be himself'. Amith's ignorance is almost all a bit much, and one wants to shake him into awareness long before he comes to terms with his homosexuality.

It is not until about a third of the way into the novel that Amrith's long-lost Canadian cousin, Niresh, is introduced. Two years older than Amrith, Niresh is a gregarious, curious spark, given to hyperbole and prevarication. He makes his younger cousin feel wanted, and in turn, Amrith unknowingly begins to fall in love with him. Amrith sees his cousin naked and becomes aroused, and lashes out at his female cousins when they attempt to manipulate Niresh's time. Amrith, so caught up in his increasingly tumultuous world, eventually loses his focus – and the part of Desdemona – and violently gives in to his jealousy. But the truth will out: Niresh reveals how his life in Canada is quite miserable, and after Niresh returns to Canada, the besotted Amrith realises that he, like Lucien, is gay. Amrith keenly feels his isolation but is not without hope.

*Swimming in the Monsoon Sea* is not a novel for adults and it is easy to see why: Amrith's self-absorption and petulance are uncritically depicted qualities that any teenager might readily identify with; all others will readily lose patience with a youth as coddled and spoiled as Amrith. Yet Selvadurai's gentle unveiling of Amrith's identity accurately illustrates the slow process of coming to knowledge that any teenager, gay or otherwise, engages. Amrith's homosexuality is presented as an incontrovertible fact; he is not an object of pity, nor is his gayness shown as unwelcome — it simply is.

In his academic introduction to his collection of South Asian writing, Selvadurai puts aside the subject of gay subjectivity to discuss the trope so familiar to South Asians: the diaspora. *Story-Wallah*'s brilliant introduction argues for diasporic writing as cultural production, especially as such creativity flows from 'the space between, that marvelous open space represented by the hyphen, in which the two parts of [an author's] identity jostle and rub up against each other like tectonic plates'. Selvardurai provides a potted history of how (postcolonial) nations struggle to assert a collective identity that nevertheless cannot be inclusive of people who are different, in whatever fashion, from the national norm. Selvadurai then ties the question of national citizenry to diasporic identity, particularly as the latter complicates any attempts at resolving the former. He writes that the idea of diaspora acknowledges the act, the trauma, of migration and the fact that one cannot but be transformed in the new land. The emphasis must shift to a sense of cultural identity that is eclectic and diverse, a sense of cultural identity that is transforming itself, making itself new over and over again.

This 'continuous work in progress' not only acknowledges similarities but, importantly, differences.

In his discussion of the various writers included in the anthology – Ondaatje, Vassanji, Desai, Mukherjee, Rushdie, Krueishi, and Monica Ali among them – Selvadurai is careful to point out the problems inherent in simple explanations of the complexity that is the South Asian diaspora. Not all of the components that might fall under the potentially homogenising label that is 'diaspora' are in any way harmonious.

In the instance of Canada, for example, the disputes between Canadians who are of Indo-Caribbean background and more recent immigrants from Asia give rise, in Shani Mootoo's 'Out on Main Street', to an examination of cross-cultural experiences that often entail the maintenance of a culture's point of origin.

So too does the anthology draw attention to new writing which, in many ways, maintains a dialogue between South Asia and the new country – using South Asia as a geographical starting point – and an appreciation of modern advances in mobility in stories such as Sandip Roy's 'Auld Lang Syne'.

The anthology itself invariably juxtaposes stories which have arisen from and deal with different locales and cultures: the volume is, as Selvardurai points out, similar to a South Asian bazaar, a milieu rich in choice in which South Asia comes to resemble a map of the world.

## Drew Shaw

## Unspeakable Love: Gay and Lesbian Life in the Middle East

Brian Whitaker

SAQI, London, 2006, pb
264pp ISBN 0 8635 6819 X £14.99
www.saqibooks.com

The Middle East is rarely out of the news, yet little is known about gay and lesbian life there. Public discussions are woefully unaware of the human face of homosexuality and *Unspeakable Love* seeks to redress the ignorance. As the Middle East editor for the *Guardian*, Brian Whitaker travelled widely in the region before writing this book. Well-researched, with an extensive bibliography and useful index, it paints a poignant portrait of Middle Eastern gay and lesbian life, analyses media, literature and film depictions, engages in discourse analysis, and challenges persecutions in the name of Islam.

IslamOnline describes homo-sexuality as 'the most heinous' sin in Islam. The supervisor of its scholarly committee, the Egyptian-born academic, Yusuf al-Qaradawi, says, in a fatwa: 'This perverted act is a reversal of the natural order, a corruption of male sexuality, and a crime against the rights of females.' Such statements, understandably, offend gay rights campaigners.

However, Whitaker is critical of campaigners who oversimplify the problem and attribute it to an immutable religion and culture. 'Treating Islam, rather than social attitudes, as the main obstacle minimises hope for reform', he states. Instead, he chooses to pay attention to the sameness, rather than otherness of Arab-Islamic culture. Homosexuality, Whitaker points out, is seen overwhelmingly in the Arab-Muslim world, as it once was in the West (and still is in parts), as a choice. This 'removes any need for tolerance or

compassion towards people who are homosexual'.

Throughout the Middle East, Whitaker shows, homosexuals are considered as either mad or bad. Parental ignorance, a lack of public discussion, and hysterical newspaper reports do little to help the situation. From Beirut to Cairo, Damascus to Palestine, to 'come out' is to disgrace not only oneself but one's entire family.

Ali, from a traditional Shi'a family in Lebanon is beaten with a chair, imprisoned in a house, locked in a car boot, and threatened with death for disgracing his family. Al-Hussein, son of a wealthy Jordanian family, forced to marry, but caught kissing his male lover, is thrown down the stairs by his brother, hospitalised, then hunted down and shot in the hospital, again by his brother. Not surprisingly, most gay men remain in the closet. To disclose their sexual orientation often means being sent for psychiatric treatment.

Lesbians have an easier time, Whitaker suggests, because they are not subjected to the same sort of scrutiny. According to Laila, from Egypt, the main requirement of girls is that they do not lose their virginity or get pregnant before marriage. Thus a 'daughter's preference for women at least reassures the family that she won't bring shame on them by getting into trouble with men'. Also, women living together as 'flatmates' do not arouse much curiosity.

Attitudes are similar, Whitaker suggests, throughout the Middle East — yet circumstances differ from state to state. Egypt began a crackdown on gay life in 2001 with a police raid on the Queen Boat, a floating gay nightclub on the Nile. Dozens of gay men were arrested, gay websites were infiltrated by government agents, and the Egyptian police began a cruel campaign of not only raiding gay parties, but also setting them up — only to entrap unsuspecting victims.

**unspeakable love**

Gay and Lesbian Life
in the Middle East

Brian
Whitaker

In Saudi Arabia, where homosexuality is punishable by death, Whitaker nevertheless reports an abundance of private gay parties in Riyadh, late night cruising in cars, and three gay cafés. The shopping malls in Jeddah, meanwhile, are apparently a magnet for gay cruising.

In Iran, where homosexuality carries the death penalty, there have been public hangings. On the other hand, transsexuality is surprisingly tolerated and gender reassignment operations are commonplace.

Similarly there are appalling stories of entrapment in Palestine, where same-sex acts are illegal and gay men frequently flee to neighbouring Israel.

In the meantime, the official media, even in Beirut (the most liberal of Arab capitals, where gay life flourishes), is relentless in its condemnation of homosexuality, but the picture, Whitaker shows, is more nuanced in Arab literature and on cinema screens. From Egypt to Tunisia, there is an ongoing attempt in the creative world to depict diverse sexual realities.

Gay Muslims are an oxymoron, we learn, to Islamic scholars such as Joseph Massad of Columbia University, who views the concepts of homosexuality

(and heterosexuality) as Western imports. Whitaker accepts, with Jeffrey Weeks, that in Muslim countries 'there is no concept of "the homosexual" except where it has been imported from the West'. However, he disagrees with Massad that the promotion of gay rights by a so-called 'Gay International' is an imperialist-style 'missionary' project. Declaring 'Arab culture cannot be treated as a fossil', Whitaker says 'the issue . . . is not whether concepts such as "gay" and "sexual orientation" are foreign imports but whether they serve a useful purpose'. To 'families – puzzled, troubled and uninformed by their own society – they offer a sensible alternative to regarding sons and daughters as sinful or mad'.

The question of sin is inescapable, it seems, and to ascertain the actual position of Islam on homosexuality, Whitaker devotes much of the book to an overview of Islamic history, the Qur'an, sharia law, various *hadith*, and what can and cannot be attributed to the Prophet Mohammed. Here, he gets a little bogged down in minutia but importantly establishes 'some evidence the Prophet was aware of sexual diversity (if not by name) and was not noticeably troubled by it'.

Although Whitaker gives an invaluable account of gay and lesbian life in the Middle East, he nevertheless succumbs to an element of homo-genisation in his commentary, and this, if anything, is the book's main weak point. His view of the Middle East is extrapolated mostly from experiences in Egypt and Lebanon and tilted more towards gay than lesbian life. There are a number of generalisations, which will no doubt be challenged in years to come when Middle Eastern gays and lesbians begin to present their own stories from their own specific localities. Until then, *Unspeakable Love* is an excellent introduction to sexuality issues in the Middle East and speaks eloquently for those who have no voice and assists a process of empowerment.

## Bruce King

# Weight Loss

## Upamanyu Chatterjee

*Penguin/Viking, New Delhi, 2006, hb*
416pp ISBN 0 6700 5862 9 Rs 495
www.penguinbooksindia.com

There is so much that is hilariously awful about Upamanyu Chatterjee's main characters and the extremes of their desires and behaviour that it is tempting to reach for a term like Rabelesian; here, however, the comic focus on the body and its functions is less rebellious than a sign of lack of balance, an unhingement. In *Weight Loss* what begins as a boy's absurd sexual fantasies becomes a short life of wildly self-destructive impulses ending at the age of thirty-nine in suicide. But, as in Chatterjee's other novels, the unlikeable central character is no worse than most of the other people in the book; like a parody of a Shakespearean tragedy the events conclude with a scene strewn with dead, mutilated, diseased, and addicted bodies.

A Chatterjee novel, made up of slightly linked episodic actions held together by the obsessions of a central character, is almost plotless. We meet Bhola at the age of eleven and Anthony, a sadistic Physical Education instructor on whom bisexual Bhola has a crush. Soon Bhola floors Anthony with an excited head butt to the groin and is expelled from school for excreting on the teacher's belongings. He is discovered exercising nude by Anin, a neighbour who is kept home from school after she tried to murder Kamala, her beautiful sister. Bhola will later have an arranged marriage to, but seldom have sex with, Kamala as he is more attracted to the smells of Moti and his wife Titli — low class, impoverished, vegetable sellers.

As flabby Bhola is obsessed by being in good shape which for him means thin, without weight, malnourished illiterate Moti becomes his erotic fantasy; Titli is one of the few women who excites him and he, a brahmin, is perversely attracted to the odorous couple. He likes dirt. Titli's whorishness adds excitement as Bhola is thrilled paying her. Bhola frantically seeks Titli after she becomes an untrained assistant for a fake medical doctor who interrupts the treatment of patients to masturbate on Titli after arousing himself with mumbo jumbo about sex as spirituality. Bhola follows them into the Himalayas where Titli eventually kills and robs the doctor. Years later after Bhola has married Kamala, he will be shot by Moti whom he has again picked up. The scandal becomes worse when Titli, now Kamala's baby's nurse, is discovered selling the baby's blood thus stimulating Bhola who immediately has sex with Titli. His semen gets on the baby's clothing, and he is assumed to be a paedophile. After a further decade of hoping for family reconciliation, he is once more at it, now with a one-eyed, fat, deformed Titli, before he cuts his wrists with ritual knives provided by Anin. That is a small taste of this insane story.

Chatterjee's novels are decentered as if they were meant to be examples of life's screwy unpredictability. The ten chapters of *Weight Loss* are of radically differing lengths, ranging from fifteen to eighty-two pages. There is little structural balance or the kind of organisation that usually supports stories. The chapter titles are mocking: 'Near-sex experiences', 'Pickmeup', 'Tie me down'. Major characters disappear for long stretches and when they reappear their status in life or career seems different although appearances are misleading and they have not really changed. People are governed by obsessions and whenever someone's life appears to have altered there will be an unexpected radical return to older traits. The extreme emotions and seemingly arbitrary structure and story are reinforced by a wide ranging vocabulary including words and phrases in Hindi, Sanskrit, even Malayalam. Chatterjee writes beautifully and the prose feels natural but it calls attention to itself by incomplete sentences,

dangling participial phrases and other examples of how English is not supposed to be written. Comparisons are unusual. Here is Bhola trailing a fat smelly female teacher during a school picnic in a public park:

> hypnotised by her hips swaying like a duck's in skintight white slacks, he as helpless and out of control as one of the stray dog suitors around a bitch on heat in a neighbourhood rubbish dump.

Such nihilism not only supports the comedy, but is also part of the significance. Like many satirists Chatterjee has a conservative streak. His India lacks shared values or the consistency of actions and morals. The problem is not cultural conflict, although modernisation is a major cause of such instability and anarchy, as Chatterjee mocks the contradictions basic to Hindu philosophy. The words 'weight loss' increasingly take on a spiritual significance, first as a healthy body supporting a healthy mind, then as an approach to spiritual weightlessness. The novel is filled with Hindu metaphysics twisted into justifications for lust:

> he would sink into the scalding morass and then burn, burn; he would at last emerge in another life, pale, whittled down to the bone, thin and light, bleached of all desire.

As for Bhola's passion for Anthony and Moti and his bisexuality:

> Think of Shiva as Ardhanarishvara, fused with the form of his consort Parvati. Think of Krishna, who as the godhead is the one true male entity and the world and its creatures are all female in principle created for his pleasure. In the mundane world too, all men and women combine the same duality. One is complete when one accepts within oneself the qualities of both genders.

*Weight Loss* brings to mind the fractured late allegories R K Narayan or the questing Brahminism of U R Anantha Murthy's *Samskara: A Rite for a Dead Man*. But whereas both earlier writers assume that a supportive system exists although it is under stress, Chatterjee writes parody and farce using Hindu symbolism in ironic pastiche. Bhola's vision is similar to that of the fake doctor who excited himself while proclaiming that sperm is the One. He likes to twist philosophy upside down by getting the words but not the intent right. If resisting worldly temptations is troubling then give in immediately.

Although Chatterjee's novels so far have been about an India unanchored from moral duty and purpose the stories have a pattern. A member of the English-speaking elite slacks off, behaving outrageously until he is long past amusing. Almost unnoticeably the story changes as events and explanations are presented less directly and fewer reasons given for what occurs, but by the conclusion it can be implied that the anti-hero is one of many signs that things are badly out of joint in the state of India. In *English, August* (1988) Agastya Sen, a recent university graduate and son of a Governor, scores high in the India Administrative Service examination but once posted to a provincial town to learn his job all he does is masturbate, smoke pot, fantasise about sex, and avoid work. Attracted by a tribal woman he, for a short time, becomes an efficient administrator until, while smoking pot with local revolutionaries, he learns that the radicals have persuaded the tribals to stay in the ruined area rather than seek a better place to camp as they would have done in the past. Moreover the Naxalites entice a friend of his into bedding an available woman and then cut off his arms as exemplary punishment for exploitation. Agastya is disgusted when other administrators laugh at his friend. Agastya Sen reappears in *The Mammaries of the Welfare State* (2000), a novel set seven years later in which a malfunctioning state bureaucracy is never reformed as everyone is governed by self-interest as is the system itself. Behind the novels is a sense of the world, work, and life being unsatisfactory, false, and without purpose. It is a feeling we all know at times but Chatterjee's main characters are from the elite and indulge in extremes of such feelings; many others in the novels are victims of social injustice who become unscrupulous to survive in a vicious culture.

The Indian family seems especially at fault; in *Weight Loss* Bhola's parents are too busy with work and play to have any time for their children. Perhaps Bhola is using a now universal 'blame the parents' cliché, but in Chatterjee's second novel, *The Last Burden* (1993), a surprisingly realistic study of a lower-middle-class family, the need for financial survival, as well as ambition, result in a depressing fragmentation as each person goes his or her own way. Yet the demands, jealousy, cruelty, and malice within the traditional joint family can be worse. This is the odd book out among Chatterjee's work and received poor reviews but it reveals how modernisation has affected India. Upamanyu Chatterjee is unpredictable but *English, August* is a minor classic and each of his subsequent novels has been interesting in unexpected ways. He is an author to follow.

© 2007 Bruce King

## Sabine Broeck

## Hotbeds: Black–White Love in Novels from the United States, Africa and the Caribbean

Pia Thielmann

*Kachere Series, Zomba, 2004, pb 395pp ISBN 9 9908 7623 1 www.sndp.org.mw/kachereseries*

In her rather sexily and allusively titled monograph, Thielmann attempts to give the reader a rather comprehensive overview of twentieth-century novels which treat the theme of bi-racial sexual and/or love relationships from various

perspectives: those written by black men, black women, white men, and white women respectively. As she writes in her introduction, this book has been autobiographically occasioned by the author's personal involvement in interracial sexual and family transgressions, and her rationale for developing arguments in the text which purposely reflect her own experience is given as follows: 'transgressions of gender and race, geographic and religious boundaries and the rewards and repercussions of such outrageous acts are "not merely personal". They are highly political, in real life, and in fiction.' Consequently, Thielmann pursues a political, as well as a literary-critical aim with her investigation, not only to demonstrate the main themes, such as the fictionalisation of interracial love, but also to trace and expose the explicit and implicit political connotations, and implications of the works. To put it in her own words:

> It can be expected that interracial love relationships in these regions experience different destinies given their respective histories and demographics — the United States being perceived as white, Africa being mainly Black, and the Caribbean relatively mixed but predominantly Black. The answers to the questions of who was and is in a power position, who was the slaver and who the enslaved, who was the colonizer and who the colonized, and how were/are identities shaped in these contexts, and under these different circumstances are also expected to leave their marks on the literary representations of interracial love by Black and white authors from the three regions.

One question that Thielmann's study raises — by including in her commentary novels addressing interracial rape, and other forms of brutally and abusively exploitative relationships — but does not

thoroughly address, is the validity of the term 'transgression' as a guiding concept in and by itself. Given that sexual and emotional relationships across colour lines have taken so many different forms and shapes, and given her observation that literary representations have variously engaged both the violent and the tender facets of those entanglements, the notion of transgression seems to be too narrow a concept.

The many novels Thielmann has chosen to discuss at greater length — covering vastly different historical and cultural ground — range from Ousmane Semene's *Ô pays, mon beau peuple!* (1957) to Andre Brink's *Cape of Storms: The First Life of Adamastor* (1993); from Shand Allfrey's *The Orchid House* (1953) to Jamaica Kincaid's *The Autobiography of My Mother* (1997) and from Alice Walker's *Meridian* (1976) to *The Chaneysville Incident* (David Bradley, 1981).

Within the available space of the standard dissertation format Thielmann cannot — even for her 'featured' authors — spend more than a couple of pages on one novel, or one author. Cursorily, however, she takes us through many texts too numerous to list here (which are also listed in her impressive, twenty-page bibliography; all primary titles are mixed in with her secondary sources, so it is impossible to tell at first sight which narrative material she is dealing with altogether). This already points to what is at the same time the main strength and the main weakness of this book: its enormous wealth of primary material.

Thielmann's study is highly recommendable for every reader – politically, or aesthetically interested – who doubts prevalent literary histories of either mainstream white origins, or of black studies' ilk (male or female authored) and their overall stubborn silence on the controversial topic of interracial mixing. For those readers who want to learn more about the actual richness of novelistic treatment of interracial relationships in all their many lustful, violent, funny, ironical, tragic, melodramatic and other representations the study provides a welcome entry into the material, summarising plots and main themes of dozens of well and lesser well-known primary texts. As an aside it should be noted that in this regard, it comes all the more as a surprise and a pity that she ignores Werner Sollors' magisterial *Neither Black, nor White, Yet Both* from 1997 which, in its treatment of miscegenation also deals with an array of textualisations of interracial relationships.

Thielmann's study makes quite obvious that despite political pronunciations of race purity and political correctness from all corners, the 'hotbed' has occupied fine novelistic minds in all quarters, and we come away from her book with first glimpses at the variety of content and forms that have been tried on this subject. First glimpses — and more curiosity, to read the novels, first, and then to move on to more in-depth studies of particular representations, narrative strategies, motifs, and styles. One problematic result of Thielmann's rather indiscriminate content-orientation is that the author discusses texts of

different genres (for example, modern and postmodern novels and Harlequin style romances) without making any distinction in her judgement of their aesthetic and/or political potential. Thus, what the present monograph does not yet provide us with is more sophisticated textual analysis that would reach farther than the thematic, and more or less rather rough summaries of its chosen texts. It remains to be hoped that other scholars, biographically invested or not, will follow Thielmann's lead and produce such studies of older, and of more contemporary 'hotbeds' of/in representations.

## Francoise Ugochukwu

### Gender and Identity in the Works of Osonye Tess Onwueme

Iniobong I Uko

*Africa World Press, Trenton and Asmara, 2004*
306pp ISBN 1 5922 1274 3 $29.95
Aalbc.com/writers/africaworldpress.htm

Reading Osonye Tess Onwueme's works within the context of gender and black literary studies, Iniobong I Uko provides a critical analysis that closely identifies with her subject, facilitating an in-depth knowledge and understanding of the plays and novel scrutinised. The book is divided into seven chapters, and explores the subjects which dominate Onwueme's works — gender relations, female identity and empowerment in Africa and the diaspora. These are followed by a long interview with the playwright and a detailed chronology of her life so far. Her last play, *What Mama Said* (2003), a follow-up to *Then She Said It*, is, regrettably, only summarily introduced and omitted in the bibliography.

Uko's book briefly reviews the various theories propounded to define

and study gender relationships in Nigeria, revealing both the huge difference between Western and African feminism and Onwueme's own abhorrence for labels and classifications. The playwright's denunciation of the gulf separating middle-class urban women from their rural counterparts acknowledges a breakdown in communication as both envisage gender relationships in very different terms.

That Onwueme had the privilege of living though the experiences of several of her characters' lives, including a rural childhood, goes some way to explain why the oral tradition 'naturally inhabits' her world, and also her success in portraying rural women, which is quite different to that which dominates a lot of writing by men on the subject.

The in-depth analysis of the plays combines their relevance to Nigerian society with their author's critical evaluation of relationships, such as her challenging of the status quo and her confrontation with the daily realities of wife and motherhood. This reveals Onwueme's commitment as an artist to the task of chronicling social contexts while at the same time suggesting 'what is useful for the people', covering such domestic issues as parenting, female education and marriage, polygamy, the preference for male children along with political ones like women's associations, female muteness, class consciousness and avarice. Her 1986 plays in particular are overt statements on Nigerian society at the time and a condemnation of a system 'that perpetuates class consciousness [and] oppression'. The book suggests her play *Wazobia* as a summation of Onwueme's message and presents it as a metaphor for unity, love and hope for a people – who symbolise Nigeria – while also addressing problems of domination and subservience, particularly the religious, ethnical and linguistic fragmentation of southern Nigeria.

Onwueme's global concerns are expressed in Chapter Five, which focuses on African American women and the diaspora. This chapter revisits the 'back-to-Africa' motif, addressing the question of dual personality and double heritage for African Americans, and insists on Onwueme's message that 'Africa and Africans in the Diaspora need to understand themselves before any form of unity can be achieved', an idea Onwueme explored through the technique of 'blended characterisation' and the twinning of characters from America and Africa. Onwueme's plays, such as *A Hen too Soon* (1983), *The Desert Encroaches* (1985), *The Broken* (1986) and *Shakara Dance-Hall Queen* (2000) are shown as projecting this vision, exploring the issues of slavery and racism and representing 'an update on the state of racial relationships in the US'.

Chapter Seven starts with an overview of African oral literature and places Onwueme's novel within a folktale genre, emphasising the author's storytelling skills and renewing the traditional theme she experimented with some twenty years before. The supremacy of storytelling is highlighted by the subtitle of the novel, *Why the Elephant Has no Butt*: 'stories mother turkey told her children — adapted from the African-igbo original'. The author

considers this novel as 'an interesting milestone in the development of Onwueme as a writer' and this explains why she chose to keep it for the last chapter, although it was published two years before the last plays. Uko views the novel as 'an extensive session of counselling', meant to improve youth socialisation and skilfully analyses the book to show its relevance in the author's oeuvre which, in sum, Uko considers to be a bold attempt to demystify womanhood while at the same time envision a new type of woman.

Generous quotes from Onwueme's plays allow her skill in bending the English language in conjunction with the structures of her mother tongue to show through. The book unearths her creative skills, in particular 'her bold experimentation with forms and techniques' such as her use of dreams, flashbacks and suspense and her use of humour, sarcasm, ridicule, witty double-entendres and metaphors. Writing with an American audience in mind, the playwright nevertheless uses proverbs and local colour, giving readers a flavour of the Nigerian multilingual situation with her frequent use of slang expressions, street language and the pidgin English she would have learnt at home in the Niger Delta.

Uko also discusses Onwueme's debt both to the oral tradition already mentioned and to other playwrights like Bertolt Brecht, Ngugi wa Thiong'o, Sembene Ousmane and Femi Osofisan, especially their roles in building peoples' theatres, largely didactic in purpose, and their identification with the oppressed and under-represented through flexible use of language, imagery and setting.

The highlight of the book is undoubtedly Uko's face-to-face interview with Onwueme, supplemented by telephone conversations and e-mails covering the months of June to October 2003. This very complete and lively account sets the book apart, clarifying a lot of issues 'in [Okwueme's] own words' while introducing readers to a vibrant, passionate and surprisingly traditional

lady who fights for female education while taking her role as a wife and a mother very seriously.

Considering that 'it is difficult to conceive of an identity for the African woman outside the context of marriage', and at a time when a new vibrant Nigerian market of self publishing emerges, subverting current publishing hurdles, Onwueme considers herself a world writer 'in search of an audience'. Her wish is that Western scholars and critics will realise that Africa is moving fast and that behind Achebe and Soyinka, many more writers, several of them female, are waiting to be recognised beyond the African literary scene. Uko's book certainly goes a long way in successfully promoting Onwueme's works.

## *Annie Paul*

## Art of the Caribbean: Selection of Postcards and Text

Anne Walmsley

*The Goodwill Art Service Ltd, Oxford, 2003, folder, £23.50*
www.goodwillart.com

This selection of artwork from the Caribbean, reproduced on postcards along with an accompanying text, is an innovative and enterprising project. Designed to be used in school classrooms it is a valuable gift to the children of the Caribbean diaspora from one of its most enduring expatriate cultural historians and educators, Anne Walmsley. *Art of the Caribbean* would seem to be the latter-day counterpart in visual art to *The Sun's Eye*, an anthology of West Indian writing for young readers published by Walmsley in 1968. Walmsley, who taught English for three years in a rural secondary school in Jamaica in the early 1960s is also well known for documenting the life and times of CAM, the Caribbean Artists' Movement, which started in London in the sixties and included many of the Anglophone Caribbean's most prominent writers, poets and artists in its membership.

Oddly enough, considering that it is quite normal to think about 'West Indian' literature, visual art in the Caribbean has resisted identification as a regional entity; instead it remains balkanised with each tiny island jealously constructing its own 'national' art history. Thus you are confronted with Jamaican art, Barbadian art, Trinidadian art or Haitian and Cuban art, the latter two being the giants among the art worlds of the region. Walmsley's *Art of the Caribbean* therefore administers a much needed palliative to the situation although sadly the common ground it assumes is felt and honoured more in the diaspora than in the competitive home territories which have steadfastly defied integration thus far.

The section titled 'Caribbean Art History' with which the text opens fluidly spins a carefully compiled set of facts spanning eight centuries into a regional narrative supporting the idea that art, as expressed in the petroglyphs, pictographs, basketry and pottery of the Tainos who once inhabited the area, was indigenous to the territory. All the same there are no visible landmarks with which to illuminate this native art terrain in the centuries preceding the arrival of the Spanish in 1492 who brought with them European traditions of art, mainly enlisted however, for religious purposes. Walmsley then provides individual histories for colonial Cuba and Saint Domingue which include brief references to twentieth-century art historical events and personages in these countries.

Some fascinating sidelights are thrown up in the process such as the fact that the earliest traces of Caribbean Creole culture first appeared in Cuba, 'notably the fusion of Catholic and African religions in *santera* (sic), its all-pervasive religious practice'. In Haiti we are told, the painting tradition was in full swing by the mid-nineteenth century with thirty Haitian artists 'at work' whose 'portrait subjects ... were blacks and mulattos who formed the country's new elite'. Walmsley attributes this to Henri

Christophe, first black king of northern Haiti who commissioned Englishman Richard Evans to paint his portrait and to establish an academy of painting, drawing and art instruction in schools. Likewise in Port-au-Prince, Walmsley suggests, the ruler of southern Haiti, Alexandre Pétion, hired French artists to do much the same. This is particularly interesting because the story we hear more often is that Haiti's prodigious art production is due to the intervention of 'visiting American' Dewitt Peters who set up the Centre d'Art in 1944, more than a hundred years later.

As Walmsley states up-front her project has a special focus on the Anglophone Caribbean. The Dutch Antilles therefore are summarily dealt with before the author proceeds to the substantive part of her thesis: the British West Indies or the English-speaking Caribbean. Walmsley euphemistically describes how the British had been trading in the West Indies from the mid-sixteenth century as 'privately sponsored buccaneers, who raided Spanish ships'. Gradually winning territories from the Spanish and the Dutch the British, 'who were the first to establish sugar-cane plantations, import Africans and practice slavery on a large scale', dominated the Caribbean by the late eighteenth century.

The practice of slavery introduced the cultural traditions of slaves to the region and Walmsley discusses the African contribution to art, evident in the tradition of domestic pottery to be found in Jamaica and in festival traditions such as Jonkonnu and Carnival. Indian labourers who were brought to the region after Emancipation 'to ensure continued productivity on the sugar estates' made their contribution to art in the Caribbean as well but according to Walmsley there was no evidence of European painting and sculpture being made in the region before the late eighteenth century despite the occasional visiting European artist. In contrast to Cuba and Haiti which enjoyed relatively long periods of 'heavily colonial, artistic activity' Western forms of art were virtually without precedent in places such as

Jamaica, Barbados, Trinidad and Guyana.

This sets the stage for the grand entrance of Edna Manley who arrives in Jamaica from England in 1922 supposedly bringing modern art with her. Although her first solo show in Kingston only takes place in 1938 the National Gallery of Jamaica's version of Jamaican art history dates the beginning of its so-called art movement to the year of her arrival in the island when she was only twenty-two and had barely begun practicing as an artist. In fact, as in Barbados and Trinidad, significant activity in Jamaican visual art only manifested itself in the late 1930s and early 1940s, a time of burgeoning nationalism and simmering social and political unrest in the region.

One of the most curious features of Jamaica's National Gallery is the official distinction it makes between what it calls 'mainstream' artists and the subaltern 'intuitives', an uneasy typology that Walmsley rightly fingers as divisive. The distinction is made between mainstream artists who are the products of formal training in art and self-taught artists without any such training who are commonly referred to as 'primitives', 'naïves' or 'outsiders' in mainstream art history. While a big deal is made of the fact that the National Gallery disdains such terms preferring instead the less derogatory sounding label 'intuitive' nothing much is changed as the operational logic behind the labels ultimately remains the same. What does it mean that a region that is itself outside the mainstream insists on recreating a mainstream for itself? Trinidadian artist Eddie Bowen for instance once asked if all Caribbean artists were not in essence 'outsider' artists in relation to the Euro-American canon. Needless to say the Jamaican curatoriat does not perturb itself with such questions pointing out that the creation of such a category actually enabled visibility and acceptance for the untrained or spontaneous artist. Ironically many of Jamaica's best-known artists, as Walmsley points out, fall into the 'intuitive' or self-taught category and she thinks are 'evidence of a continuous indigenous art tradition'. John Dunkley, claimed to be Jamaica's 'foremost' artist, famously spurned art instruction at classes held by Edna Manley and others in the late 1930s.

Brief art histories of Barbados, Guyana and Trinidad follow that of Jamaica, documenting key moments, personages, events and institutions in each country. The racial dynamics of art discourse in the region is hinted at by Walmsley's noting that art in Barbados was 'widely regarded as something done by expatriates'. Jamaica too has had more than its fair share of expatriate artists, curators and educators involved in the production of visual art. This, coupled with the fact that visual art tends to be, in any society, a rarefied activity almost exclusively controlled by its elites means that despite the best intentions of those involved there is an unhealthy disconnect between the art scene in Jamaica and the average citizen. The easy assimilation of expatriates into Caribbean art worlds contrasts strongly with the West Indian literary canon which far from admitting expatriates, even balks at the inclusion of white West Indian writers, who are viewed as being culturally incapable of authentically representing populations that are largely black or non-white.

Walmsley ends her text by briefly examining Caribbean-born artists in Britain; her poignant inclusion of Denzil Forrester's 'The Burial of Winston Rose' deftly brings in the diaspora and the spiritual alienation suffered by Caribbean immigrants. The classroom activities included at the back as well as the notes on each individual postcard provide a rich amalgam of art-related learning which would provide children with a strong sense of the visual art of the region. The text is illustrated with line drawings and black and white reproductions while the postcards reproduce the artworks in full colour. Though designed mainly for children in the Caribbean diaspora, particularly in Britain, *Art in the Caribbean* would also greatly enhance visual art curricula in the Anglophone Caribbean, promoting a regional sense among local children

currently locked into rigid national narratives. For that matter this art package published by the Goodwill Art Service could serve as an engaging introduction to Caribbean art for many an adult interested in exploring such subjects. It is true that Walmsley's approach to art is more traditional than contemporary with new media such as video and installation left out in the cold. Except for this and a very small number of typos and errors (the date for *This Land of Mine* by Barbadian artist Annalee Davis, born in 1963, is given as 1966 when she would have been three years old), this innovative pack of materials is a pedagogical tool of great value.

## Bill Schwarz

### A Meeting of the Continents: The International Book Fair of Radical Black and Third World Books Revisited: History, Memories, Organisation, and Programmes 1982–1995

Sarah White, Roxy Harris and Sharmilla Beezmohun, eds

*New Beacon Books and George Padmore Institute, London, 2005, hb 560pp ISBN 1 8732 0118 4 £25.00 www.georgepadmoreinstitute.org/ newbeacon.asp*

Older readers of *Wasafiri* will remember the successive International Book Fairs of Radical Black and Third World Books. They were an inspiration for an entire generation in the UK and much further afield. It is impossible to imagine the contemporary intellectual world in Britain without grasping the significance of the Black and Third World Book Fair. The very possibility of thinking in terms of a black aesthetic; the idea that writers from the former colonies possessed the imagination and capacity to 'write back'; the bringing to life of a rich variant of

black feminisms; the notion that continents might 'meet' and that they could do so through the articulation of a democratic politics and literature: the Book Fairs did not exactly invent these modes of thought and being – that would be claiming too much – but they gave them form and voice, and did so with a distinctive drive, energy and implacable generosity.

Too often the story of the coming of 'other' literatures to the UK is presented in too abstract a voice. The conventional story begins, as if by an immaculate conception, with Salman Rushdie's *Midnight's Children* and continues with the publication of a string of more great writers, publicly accredited by publishers and reviewers. In this version of things, the species of postcolonial theory which typifies the academy becomes the begetter of all that this transformation represents, as if the theory enabled the practice to happen. It is no disrespect to Rushdie, nor to those who have followed in his footsteps, nor indeed to those (myself included) who teach postcolonialism in the universities, to suggest that this is a lop-sided conception of a more complex, more visceral history: and one in which the Book Fairs played an indispensable role.

In the inauspicious month of April 1982 – the exact moment of the war with Argentina: a terrible time when the instincts of the old empire cut through into the present – three publishers, Bogle-L'Ouverture, New Beacon and Race Today, launched the first of the fairs, opened by the esteemed and by this date venerable figure of C L R James. Twelve further events followed, the enterprise coming to a close in 1995. These later occasions moved out from London to Manchester, Leeds and Glasgow, and in 1987 and 1988 they were linked to the Caribbean People's International Book Fair and the Book Fair Festival.

From the vantage of current political imperatives the Book Fairs were resolutely old school, working to operate outside the commodified world of publishing, universities and state support. The idea of a book *fair* is a common one. But in practice most book fairs can be dull affairs, consumed by the cult of celebrity, with very little sense of popular festivity. Exactly the contrary was true of the Black and Third World Book Fairs. They were popular in every sense of the word, embracing a vision of the world turned upside down or (as Fanon put it) a vision in which the last shall be first, and the first last. Those attending from the UK or overseas could count on no financial support and no swanky hotels: they came under their own steam, and relied on the goodwill of friends and supporters in Britain to care for them when they arrived.

The documents collected together in the current volume represent an archival treasure. The programmes are reproduced here, with a range of adjacent documentation and various retrospective judgements. The volume represents an effervescent cultural and political history of a key moment, or conjuncture, of our recent history. From it can be discerned the connections between the literary imagination and the hard process of politics. For all the excitement of new voices assuming public authority, though, political defeat and tragedy are never far distant. In particular, the destruction of the New Jewel Movement in Grenada and, nearer to home for UK readers, the deaths of the New Cross teenagers darken the pages of what otherwise represents a commemorative volume. Even so, that such a publication can be produced in these times is credit not only to the indefatigable editors, but so too to that stalwart of good thinking, the Rowntree Trust, which underwrote at least some of the costs of publication.

As I well remember, continents did meet in the Book Fairs. From the start they sought to be international and, so far as a shoestring organisation allowed, this they achieved. But their genealogy was more particular. The entire venture represented a peculiarly Caribbean enterprise. Of the sixty or so speakers invited to the opening conference more than half came from the Caribbean, or had a close Caribbean connection. That James should have been accorded the role of presiding maestro of the first Fair

in 1982 – appropriating the magic of Prospero while refusing to relinquish the identification with Caliban – was entirely appropriate. The Caribbean genealogy is part of a larger intellectual history of the diaspora in Britain, stretching back to the work of James and George Padmore in London in the 1930s, drawing in the Manchester Pan-African meeting in 1945, embracing the memory of Claudia Jones and her *West Indian Gazette* at the end of the fifties, and taking us to the Caribbean Artists' Movement of the sixties and seventies. The Book Fairs were an extension of this deeper history, inventing new forms while consciously continuing a longer tradition.

To say this is not to question the integrity of the commitment to the internationalism of the organisers — this cannot be doubted. But it highlights a specific history of the diasporic Caribbean in Britain — a story whose full panorama we have yet to get in focus. Yet it is not only the Caribbean, or the diasporic Caribbean. Within this formation, Trinidad and Tobago can claim a privileged position. And (becoming ever more local) within *this* formation, the figure of John La Rose stands out as an inspiration through whom much of this happened.

La Rose was the founder of New Beacon Books and of its publishing arm. He was director of the Book Fair. He was a co-founder of the Caribbean Artists' Movement. He involved himself in a myriad of popular-political campaigns in the nearly fifty years of his stay in the UK. His ties to the Oil Workers of Trinidad remained close throughout. He was, in sum, a central presence in the making of contemporary black Britain.

There are now many stories which tell us of the evolution of the Caribbean migration to Britain, which describe survival and teeth-gritting accommodation. There are different strands to this, as migrants made their own choices. La Rose's position, we can see in retrospect, was clear throughout: *his* strategy was based on the commitment to the autonomy of a popular migrant politics. His was not a politics built upon achieving access to

the social institutions of British life. Access seemed to have bored him, and carried too many dangers. Rather than building a life seeking entry to what Britain offered La Rose – with good grace, intelligence and much humour – determined to create new spheres of activity, close to the lived migrant experience, which themselves would flourish and, in time, require native Britons to heed, to understand and ultimately to learn from.

The Radical Black and Third World Book Fairs represented one such venture. Much that we now understand simply as literature or culture was first incubated there. Through the impetus of the Caribbean migrant experience Britain was opened up to a new world. In La Rose the tradition of James, Padmore and Claudia Jones continued into a new age. Through, listening to these Trinidadians Britons, and others, could imagine themselves anew.

## Leila Kamali

### Brown Eyes: A Selection of Creative Expressions by Black and Mixed-Race Women
Nicole Moore, ed.

*Matador, Leicester, 2005, pb*
268pp ISBN 1 9052 3714 6 £9.99
www.troubadour.co.uk/matador

According to the editor Nicole Moore, 'The aim [of *Brown Eyes*] was to discover new and diverse talent, ensure representation and act as a medium for black and mixed-race women [in Britain] to speak out and reach a much wider audience.' This anthology, which appears to have been compiled, in part, from writers' workshops, consists of poems and essays, as well as interviews in which contributors elucidate their approaches to their work. Moore's editorial strategy thus establishes a promising counterpoint from which dialogue might emerge, not only between writers, but also from the shifts in pace and inflection which emerge between diverse forms.

There are indeed moments of inspiration to be enjoyed here, particularly in the sensitive illumination of historical memory in a poem such as Maggie Harris's 'Origins':

> Yes, track me the scent of my
>     skin on a coast of Paramaribo
> where a trade wind blowing its
>     precious cargo
> doesn't know that one day
>     they'll build rockets
> from behind those trees and
>     aim for the moon

The memory of slavery resounds powerfully in some pieces, nowhere more so than in Louise Hercules' poem, 'The Quay', as she evokes 'the gaze of those so ready to slay your hand from mine', or as Kimberly Trusty imagines a 'slave ship/turned upside down/on the banks of the Ohio River'. The movement, both historical and current, of lives lived across diverse terrains, is vividly felt in a poem such as 'Home' by Tolu Melissa Carew:

> When I put my arms around my
>     lover
> And I kiss his face
> I am home . . .
> Not home in London but in
>     Lagos . . .
> I am in Victoria Island, Biaduo.
> I am 10.

Less exciting is the frequent appearance throughout this volume of bland mythologisations of African matriarchs, and equally, of matriarchal Africas. Contributors wax lyrical on this well-worn theme, from a simple glorification of black femininity, such as Lynda Wireko's 'Woman black woman,/I see God's beauty within you', to an abstraction of the figure of the black mother with a generalised African motherland in Amanda Epé's 'The Diaspora':

> She stands central and
>     large . . .
> Her dispersed seed across the
>     oceans
> Evolved into a beautiful life

The exaltation of the matriarch forms only part of the very large dose of essentialising racial 'pride' which this volume delivers, conveyed with a plentiful array of clichés and rhymes such as 'The black race is Ace/We all go through hard times./But nothing can take away our gifted minds.'

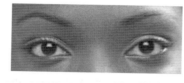
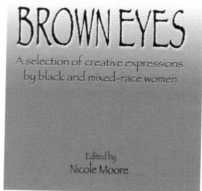

Nicole Moore, in her Introduction, writes that 'Brown Eyes is meant to celebrate, reflect upon and embrace our diverse female identities and the common-thread that unites us living the UK experience.' The terms 'black' and 'mixed-race' are used in the context of this collection to refer to 'women from African and African-Caribbean backgrounds'; and diversity and commonality, which Moore so rightly identifies as values which should be held in balance in such an anthology as this, are indeed broadly represented. Yet the volume is divided into sections with titles such as 'Cinnamon: What's it like being us?', 'Chocolate: Who do you think we are?', and 'Beige: When will our skin colour be just a colour?' Isn't there something deeply

questionable about representing identity through food analogies, let alone about grading skin tone as if it were a selection of paint swatches? There is a distinct sense that Moore guides the focus of the volume into something of a cul-de-sac based upon her own rather fixed understanding of cultural identity, and this can elicit a certain (perhaps unintentionally) bemused candour such as is shown by Daniella Blechler: 'I don't go out and look for books that are by mixed-race women. I look for books that appeal to me.'

In her own poem, which begins with the line 'Colour, hue, I just love you', Moore surmises that:

> it's more than just a colour
> That creates fear amongst
>     ignorance
> It's the unknown face
> Of difference

Moore's concluding comment to her own essay, elsewhere in the volume, reads: 'It isn't problematic that mixed-race people are bi-racial or of dual-heritage; it is that there is so much silence, ignorance and racism.' The reader is forced to ask whether simply naming a problem in this way really does the work that 'creative expression' surely can, of reconciling marginalised subjects with a society which seeks to exclude or devalue them.

At times, this volume provides useful responses to the challenge which seems to be set in its very title. Portia Msimang demonstrates awareness of the differential which often exists between the terms 'black' and 'mixed-race' as they function in everyday use:

> Here and now, we are in a
> position to abandon the
> scientifically discredited, morally
> repugnant philosophies, which
> have elsewhere demonstrably
> decreased the vulnerability of
> those who are willing to embrace
> their status as 'mulatto',

'coloured', or 'mixed-race'... When I look in the mirror, a black woman reflects back at me. In those eyes, there is a slight weariness from 30 years of arguing to be allowed to be black... The reflection I see in windows... walks with head held high because inside it, I carry my heritage, the unshakeable belief in world citizenship, with great care.

Dorothy Cornibert du Boulay, similarly, recognises the power of an identification which transcends uncomfortable racial hierarchies, when she asserts, 'I realised that black was global'. Signifiers, like poetry itself, can transcend distances and divisions in order to assert a place for marginalised identities within a continuum of human diversity, and it is clearly in this way that the use of any particular identification, whether 'black' or 'mixed-race', is most liberating and productive. Sheree Mack puts it nicely: 'I'm a "mixness". There is no box to tick for that.' Emma Louise Felicia Hopkins's poem, 'All I Can Want is What There Is', can similarly be seen as a clever response to this volume's overarching focus on skin tone:

> All colours treat lives like
>   shades
> Like safe bait
> Tight in their skin, possessive
>   in pace
> All features fester
> And colour is my self-defence

*Brown Eyes* fulfils its promise of offering exposure to some talented writers, but if Moore proceeds with her professed plan to produce two further such volumes, she would be well advised to enforce slightly more stringent 'quality control' over contributions, as well as undertaking a careful consideration of what it means to truly represent diversity.

## Susanne Mühleisen

### Linton Kwesi Johnson Live in Paris with the Dennis Bovell Dub Band

*LKJ Records, London, 2005, CD*

LKJ CD 022, LKJ DVD 001
www.lkjrecords.com

When in 1978, the black British poet, music journalist and political activist Linton Kwesi Johnson released his first album *Dread Beat and Blood*, his audience was not aware, as Christian Habekost recounts in *Verbal Riddim*, that 'this was dub poetry captured on a record for the first time'. It was clear from the very beginning, however, that this was something new — new in style and music, as well as in the content of the lyrics. Spoken words on reggae beat ('toasting') had already been popular in the DJ scene in Jamaica throughout the 1970s, but Linton Kwesi Johnson's debut work revealed an entirely new poetic and political quality and had its own distinctive British flavour. Johnson's powerful spoken poetry over reggae sounds has since become almost synonymous with Dub Poetry, a term and style for which he is widely regarded as the founding figure.

The DVD – *Linton Kwesi Johnson live in Paris with the Dennis Bovell Dub Band*, recorded at a concert at the Zenith, Paris, in 2003 – marks the twenty-fifth anniversary of the release of *Dread Beat and Blood*, and hence the silver jubilee of this unique relationship between poetry and music. In the first three performances – 'Di Eagle An Di Bear', 'Want Fi Goh Rave' and 'Sonny's Lettah' – the artist presents a taste of his works from different albums like *Mekkin Histri* and *Dread Beat and Blood* across the last twenty-five years. The next section is clearly dedicated to early works with a strong agenda of political activism.

In an atmosphere of constant talk about the 'fight against terrorism', Johnson reminds his audience that the so-called ethnic minorities of Europe have known this fight for decades — the fight against the terrorism of racism. Thus, 'Fite Dem Back', 'Reggae Fi Peach', 'Reggae Fi Radni' and the a capella version of 'Di Great Insohreckshan' take us back to earlier struggles and events in black British history, to the 1979 murder of the anti-Nazi activist Blair Peach, to the fate of Walter Rodney, the Guyanese academic and political activist who was assassinated in 1980, as well to the Brixton riots in 1981. Songs like 'Liesense Fi Kill' about black deaths in police custody and the 'conspiracy of silence' about these matters make clear, however, that this struggle is far from won.

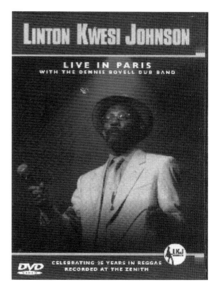

So, is 'Inglan' still the bitch she was in 1980? This old-time favourite is conspicuously absent, as are some of Johnson's more personal lyrics, such as 'Lorraine' or 'Reggae Fi Dada'. The last poem/song, however, performed after a few more classics like 'Mekkin Histri', 'Tings An Times' and 'More Time' is 'Reggae Fi Bernard', dedicated to Johnson's nephew who died in tragic circumstances in 1995. Here, it becomes perhaps most clear how the political and the personal merge in Johnson's lyrics, adding a very tender tone to the stance of political dedication.

In the packed concert atmosphere at the Zenith, Johnson presents himself in the manner which has become his trademark: in impeccable suit, tie and hat, he performs his powerful lyrics with his usual reduced movements, compelling even the excited concert audience to pay attention not only to sound and vision, but also to the content of his works. The Dennis Bovell Dub Band has become more than just the musical background support to his lyrics but is an essential part of the show and make this DVD a feast to the ears, as well as to the eyes and the mind. The sixty-minute concert recording is accompanied by a twenty-minute interview and a photo gallery. In the interview, Johnson talks about his childhood in Jamaica in the 1950s and early 1960s and the various influences on his music. 'I didn't discover music, I was born with music! From the time I heard my heart beating, I knew I had music', so he claims. But also his poetry has its roots in his early years in the Caribbean, with influences like the 'poetry of the Bible', as he told Burt Caesar in an interview, read at his grandmother's home and a later, perhaps more conscious, stimulus by the works of Caribbean poets like Edward Kamau Brathwaite. Linton Kwesi Johnson also talks about his experience of racism in Britain, after joining his mother in London at the age of eleven and his subsequent political work which began at the age of fifteen or sixteen. His further revelations about his early work in the music industry and a consequential dinner with Richard Branson in 1977, as well as an a capella recital of 'Reggae Fi Bernard' make this interview an additional asset to the concert performance on this DVD.

Linton Kwesi Johnson may well be called a living legend, being, after all, only the second living person to have been included in the Penguin Modern Classics series. His influence on the music scene is as powerful as his influence on the use of patois – or nation language, as he prefers to call it – and his way of presenting his words not only orally but also on the page has become a model for many other writers and poets. His work is also living proof of the success of black British culture in transforming British society in the past decades.

# Books Received

### Writers and Their Work: Shashi Deshpande

Amrita Bhalla

*Northcote House, Tavistock, 2006, pb*
111pp ISBN 0 7463 0947 3 £11.99

### Writers and Their Work: Anita Desai

Elaine Yee Lin Ho

*Northcote House, Tavistock, 2006, pb*
118pp ISBN 0 7463 0983 X £11.99

### The decibel Penguin Anthology: New Voices from a Diverse Culture Vol 1

*Penguin, London, 2006, pb*
183pp ISBN 0 1410 2702 9 £7.99

### Imagining Persia: Memoirs from Diaspora

Geoffrey Nash

*Grosvenor House, Guildford, 2006, pb*
157pp ISBN 1 9055 2944 9

### Street on the Hill

Anjum Hassan

*Sahitya Akademi, New Delhi, 2006, pb*
64pp ISBN 8 1260 1793 7 Rs40

### The Forward Book of Poetry 2007

*Forward Ltd and Faber & Faber,*
*London, 2006, pb*
127pp ISBN 0 5712 3448 8 £8.99

### Mazhar ul Islam: The Season of Love, Bitter Almonds and Delayed Rains: Selected Stories and Other Pieces

Christopher Shackle, ed and trans

*Sama, Karachi, 2006, hb*
262pp ISBN 9 6987 8454 4 Rs375

### Music for the Off-Key: Twelve Macabre Short Stories

Courttia Newland

*Peepal Tree Press, Leeds, 2006, pb*
168pp ISBN 1 8452 3040 X £8.99

### Halala Madiba: Nelson Mandela in Poetry

Richard Bartlett, ed

*Aflame Books, Laverstock, 2006, pb*
294pp ISBN 0 9552 3390 9 £9.95

### Reinterpreting the Haitian Revolution and its Cultural Aftershocks

Martin Munro and Elizabeth Walcott-Hackshaw, eds

*University of the West Indies Press,*
*Kingston, 2006, pb*
184pp ISBN 9 7664 0190 X

### Crossing Waters, Crossing Worlds: The African Diaspora in Indian Country

Tiya Miles and Sharon P Holland, eds

*Duke University Press, Durham,*
*2006, pb*
364pp ISBN 0 8223 3865 3 £14.99

### Mobilizing India: Women, Music and Migration Between India and Trinidad

Tejaswini Niranjana

*Duke University Press, Durham,*
*2006, pb*
271pp ISBN 0 8223 3842 4 £13.99

### At Home with Miss Vanessa

E A Markham

*Tindal Street Press, Birmingham,*
*2006, pb*
263pp ISBN 0 9551 3840 X £8.99

### The Silent Minaret

Ishtiyaq Shukri

*Jacana, Johannesburg, 2005, pb*
247pp ISBN 1 7700 9249 8 £10.95

### Island Songs

Alex Wheatle

*Allison & Busby, London, 2006, pb*
329pp ISBN 0 7490 8243 7 £7.99

*Wasafiri Vol. 22, No. 1 March 2007, pp. 89–90*
ISSN 0269-0055 print/ISSN 1747-1508 online © 2007 Wasafiri
http://www.tandf.co.uk/journals     DOI: 10.1080/02690050601097872

## My Mother Who is Me: Life Stories from Jamaican Women in New York

Jacqueline Bishop

*Africa World Press, Trenton and New Jersey, 2006, pb*
204pp ISBN 1 5922 1344 8 US$19.95

## Pink Icing and Other Stories

Pamela Mordecai

*Insomniac Press, Toronto, 2006, pb*
241pp ISBN 1 8971 7832 8 £9.95

## The Unlikely Burden and Other Stories

Dipesh Pabari and Lila Luce

*World Society for the Protection of Animals, Dar es Salaam and Sasa Sema Publications, Nairobi, 2006, pb*
135pp ISBN 9 9669 5139 3

## The Song of the Atman

Ronnie Govender

*Jacana, Johannesburg, 2006, pb*
322pp ISBN 1 7700 9186 6 £10.95

## Mirage

Kokilam Subbiah

*Orient Longman, Chennai, 2006, pb*
200pp ISBN 8 1250 3070 0 £12.95

## The Grip of Change

P Sivakami

*Orient Longman, Chennai, 2006, pb*
207pp ISBN 8 1250 3020 4 £9.95

## Under the Perfume Tree

Judy Stone, ed

*Macmillan Caribbean, Oxford, 2006, pb*
317pp ISBN 1 4050 6518 4 £5.95

## Matters of Life and Death

Lesego Malepe

*Black Coral, Columbus, 2006, pb*
243pp ISBN 1 5857 1124 1 $15.95

## Writers and Their Work: Caryl Phillips

Helen Thomas

*Northcote Press, Tavistock, 200b, pb*
100pp ISBN 0 7463 0956 2 £12.99

## Writing Madness

Flora Veit-Wild

*James Currey, Oxford, 2006, pb*
174pp ISBN 0 8525 5583 0 £14.99

## . . . and the Sirens Still Wail

Nancy Burke

*Macmillan Caribbean, Oxford, 2006, pb*
166pp ISBN 1 4050 1703 1 £5.25

## Chutney Power

Willi Chen

*Macmillan Caribbean, Oxford, 2006, pb*
162pp ISBN 1 4050 2973 0 £5.00

## Joseph – A Rasta Reggae Fable

Barbara Makeda Blake Hannah

*Macmillan Caribbean, Oxford, 2006, pb*
202pp ISBN 1 4050 6143 X £5.50

## Caribbean Dispatches: Beyond the Tourist Dream

Jane Bryce, ed

*Macmillan Caribbean, Oxford, 2006, pb*
209pp ISBN 1 4050 7136 2 £15.00

## Haunted British: The Celtic Fringe, the British Empire and De-Aglicization

Laura O'Connor

*John Hopkins University Press, Baltimore, 2006, hb*
240pp ISBN 0 8018 8433 0

# Among the Contributors

**Christopher Barnes** lives in England. His first collection of poems *Lovebites* is published by Chanticleer Press. In May 2006 he had an exhibition of concept art and poetry at Newcastle's People's Theatre and has a BBC website <ww.bbc.co.uk/tyne/gay/05/section_28.shtml>

**Kanika Batra** teaches at the University of Delhi and Loyola University Chicago. Her publications include a monograph on Caribbean poetry for the Indira Gandhi National Open University, India. Her research interests include feminist and queer theory, postcolonial and performance studies.

**Gautam Bhan** is a writer and queer rights activist based in New Delhi. He is co-editor of *Because I Have a Voice: Queer Politics in India* (Yoda Press, 2005), one of the first comprehensive anthologies of queer writing in India. He is Series Editor of *Sexualities*, an inter-disciplinary list on gender and sexuality at Yoda Press.

**Sabine Broeck** has published widely in the area of Americanisation in an international comparative perspective. She was a founding member of the University of Bremen's *INPUTS* (Institute for Postcolonial and Transcultural Studies) where she is Professor of American Studies.

**Maureen Duffy** is the acclaimed author of nineteen novels, seven poetry collections and five works of non-fiction. Her most recent novel, *Alchemy*, was published in 2005. She is said to have been Britain's first lesbian to come out in public, publishing her first openly lesbian novel, *The Microcosm*, in 1966.

**Chris Dunton** has taught in universities in Nigeria, Libya and South Africa. At present he is Professor of English and Dean of Humanities at the National University of Lesotho. He has written extensively on Nigerian literature and has recently published a collection of short stories, *Boxing* (African Books Collective).

**Maggie Gee** is the author of ten novels including *The White Family*, *The Flood* and *My Cleaner*. Her latest book is a collection of short stories entitled *The Blue*. She is the first female chair of the Royal Society of Literature and a member of the *Wasafiri* editorial board.

**Gillian Hanscombe** has published poems, fiction, articles and essays in anthologies and collections in Britain, the USA, Canada and Australia. Her books include *Between Friends*, *Sybil*, *The Glide of Her Tongue* and *Figments of a Murder*. She lives in Devon.

**Jarrod Hayes** is Associate Professor of French and Francophone studies at the University of Michigan. He is the author of *Queer Nations: Marginal Sexualities in the Maghreb* (Chicago, 2000). His essay here is part of a current book project, *Queer Roots for the Diaspora, Ghosts in the Family Tree*.

*Wasafiri Vol. 22, No. 1 March 2007, pp. 91–93*
ISSN 0269-0055 print/ISSN 1747-1508 online © 2007 Wasafiri
http://www.tandf.co.uk/journals     DOI: 10.1080/02690050601097880

**Bruce King** lives in Paris. His most recent book was the updated edition of *Three Indian Poets* (OUP, 2005). His *Internationalization of English Literature 1948–2000*, the concluding volume of the new Oxford English Literary History, is going to be republished in China.

**Linton Kwesi Johnson** is a reggae poet and recording artist. He has published six volumes of poetry and released some fifteen albums. His latest book, *Mi Revalueshanary Fren: Selected Poems* is published by Penguin.

**Jackie Kay** lives in Manchester and is a poet, novelist and short story writer. Her publications include *Trumpet*, winner of the *Guardian* Fiction Award, *Why Don't You Stop Talking* and recently the Poetry Society Recommendation *Life Mask*. Her short story collection *Wish I Was Here* was published in June 2006 by Picador. Jackie Kay is a Fellow of the Royal Society of Literature.

**Andrew Lesk** is an Assistant Professor of English at the University of Toronto, where he teaches Canadian Literature.

**Keguro Macharia** was born and raised in Nairobi, Kenya. He is currently resident in the USA, working on his doctorate in English.

**Susanne Mühleisen** is Professor of English linguistics at the University of Bayreuth, Germany. Her main research interests are Creole Studies, Black British Englishes, as well as translation and intercultural communication. She is the author of *Creole Discourse: Exploring Prestige Formation and Change across Caribbean English-lexicon Creoles* (2002) and co-editor of *Politeness and Face in Caribbean Creoles* (2005).

**Suniti Namjoshi** has worked for the Indian Administrative Service and in academic posts in India and Canada. She now lives in Devon. Her books include *Feminist Fables*, *Saint Suniti and the Dragon*, *Building Babel* and *Goja: An Autobiographical Myth*. *Sycorax: New Fables and Poems* is to be published by Penguin India. She has also published several children's books in the 'Aditi' series with Tulika Publishers, India.

**Denise deCaires Narain** is a Senior lecturer in English at the University of Sussex. She has published widely on Caribbean women's writing and is currently completing a monograph on Olive Senior as well as research for a critical study of contemporary postcolonial women's writing.

**Annie Paul** is a writer and critic based at the University of the West Indies, Mona, where she is head of the Publications Section at the Sir Arthur Lewis Institute of Social and Economic Studies. She is Associate editor of *Small Axe* (Indiana University Press) and of the *Cultures and Globalization Series* (Sage, London).

**Ian Iqbal Rashid** was born in Dar es Salaam and raised in Toronto, but now lives in London. He is the author of three volumes of poetry, *Black Markets, White Boyfriends (and other Acts of Elision)*, *Song of Sabu* and *The Heat Yesterday*. His first feature film, *Touch of Pink*, was distributed internationally by Sony Picture Classics in 2004.

**Sara Salih** is Associate Professor in English at the University of Toronto. She is currently working on a book about representations of 'brown' women in Jamaica and England from the Abolition era to the present day, to be published by Routledge.

**Bill Schwarz** is Reader in Postcolonial Studies in the School of English and Drama at Queen Mary, University of London. Most recently he has edited *West Indian Intellectuals in Britain* and is currently working on two critical collections, one on George Lamming, the other on Earl Lovelace.

**Drew Shaw** is a graduate of the University of Toronto, the University of Cape Town and Queen Mary, University of London. His doctoral thesis contains the first comprehensive analysis of lesbian, gay, bisexual and transgendered themes and their significance in Zimbabwean writing. He is currently a Visiting Lecturer for the NILE programme at the Institute of English Studies, University of London.

**Caroline Smith** is a writer and performer. She is Arts Editor of *Attitude* and has previously contributed to *Creative Camera* and *Women's Art Magazine* in London as well as *Black Book* and *Photo District News* in New York. She is Senior Lecturer in Media Writing at Greenwich University.

**Saradha Soobrayen** is the Poetry Editor of *Chroma: A Queer Literary Journal*. Her short fiction is published in *KIN: New fiction by Black and Asian Women* (Serpent's Tail 2003). She received an Eric Gregory award for poetry in 2004. She lives in London, where she facilitates writing workshops and writes poetry reviews.

**Françoise Ugochukwu** has been lecturing in Higher Education in Nigeria, France and the UK for over thirty years and is a specialist in Comparative Literature (African Literatures and Cultures and Ethnolinguistics). She was awarded the *Chevalier des Palmes Académiques* in 1994 for her pioneering work and her longstanding contribution to the strengthening of cultural and educational ties between France and Nigeria.

**d'bi young** is a Jamaican-Canadian dub poet, actor and playwright who believes in life, love and 'revolushun'. She has published extensively including her premiere book of poetry, *art on black*, her first play co-written with Naila Blevett, *yagayah*, and her Dora award-winning one-woman play *blood.claat*, which will premier in London in the autumn of 2007.

# African and Black Diaspora:
## *An International Journal*
### NEW FOR 2008

## CALL FOR PAPERS

This is the first academic journal that directly addresses the needs of scholars working in the important field of African diaspora studies. It will advance the analytical and interrogative discourses that constitute this distinctive interdisciplinary study into the deterritorialised and transnational nature of the African and Black diaspora.

Beyond essentialist modes of theorizing, the journal will locate the movement of African descended populations (geographical, cultural, social, political and psychological) in the context of globalized and transnational spaces by emphasizing the centrality of African and black diaspora.

### Editors

**Fassil Demissie,** *Public Policy Studies, DePaul University, Chicago USA*
**Sandra Jackson,** *Center for Black Diaspora, DePaul University, Chicago USA*
**Abebe Zegeye,** *University of South Africa, Pretoria, South Africa*

### Editorial Board

### *Supported by an International Advisory Board*

### Submission Details

Please send all submissions to the editors:
**Fassil Demissie,** *Public Policy Studies, DePaul University, 2352 N. Clifton Ave, Chicago, IL 60614,*
fdemissi@depaul.edu
**Sandra Jackson,** *Center for Black Diaspora, DePaul University, 2320 N. Kenmore Ave, Chicago, IL 60614,*
sjackson@depaul.edu
**Abebe Zegeya,** *The School for Graduate Studies, University of South Africa, PO Box 392, Pretoria 0003, South Africa,* zegeya@unisa.ac.zaa

For further information on *African & Black Diaspora: An International Journal* please contact alexis.goodyear@tandf.co.uk

View further journal information at:
## www.tandf.co.uk/journals

# Notes for Contributors

*Wasafiri* welcomes original contributions from poets, fiction writers and critics from all cultural backgrounds. We are particularly interested in publishing informed and lively essays on the work of established and emerging writers or interviews with them. Submitted work is peer-reviewed by established writers, critics and academics, ensuring *Wasafiri*'s long reputation for forging new perspectives and publishing the best in contemporary writing today. A modest fee is paid by *Wasafiri* to reviewers and those whose creative work is accepted. All material should be sent direct to: **Susheila Nasta, Editor, Wasafiri, The Open University, 1–11 Hawley Crescent, Camden Town, London NW1 8NP.** Books being sent for review should be marked for the attention of the **Reviews Editor**.

Manuscripts should be submitted according to the following:

## General

- Two hard (paper) copies and an electronic copy of your work are required. Please ensure hard copies are firmly stapled together and marked MS in the top right hand corner. If you wish to have your MS returned enclose a self-addressed envelope.
- Length: Articles/Fiction (5000–6000 words); Review Essay (up to 2500 words).
- Include Author(s) names(s) and affiliation, full correspondence address, fax, landline, mobile, and email for author (top right hand corner of first page). Include short biography in submission letter, 50 words (and as electronic file). Please make sure that the hard copy is an exact printout of the electronic version.

## Format

- Type/print on A4 plain white paper, one side only, double spaced.
- Font: Times New Roman, 12 pt, align left, unjustified.
- Title: align left 20 pt, Sub title 16 pt followed by author(s) name(s) 14 pt.
- No centring throughout text, no headers or footers, no page numbers.
- Single space after full stops.
- Tab for paragraph indent — 0.5 cm, no space between paragraphs. Do not indent first paragraph, or first paragraph of a new section. Leave one line space before a new section.
- Use parenthetical referencing for bibliographical material. Other notes (which should be kept to a minimum) should appear as endnotes, numbered consecutively in Arabic numerals. Any notes should be part of the main body text and be typed normally at the end of the text. These should be kept to a minimum. Do not use the footnote or endnote facility of your WP program. Do not use auto numbering facility.
- Picture captions: All slides, transparencies or photographs should be numbered and where known, the photographer's name should be given. If the picture is of a work of art then artist, title, date, dimensions, medium photo credit should be given, in that order. Electronic picture files should be provided as 300dpi tif files. These files should be burnt onto a CD and sent with the manuscript. Please mark in the text of the manuscript the approximate position of all images, highlight in red.

## References

The magazine uses a slightly modified version of the format advocated by Joseph Gibaldi and Walter Achtert, *MLA Handbook for Writers of Research Papers*. The Modern Languages Association of America, 1999 (www.mla.org). References conform to the MLA style with the following exceptions:

- Use single quotes (not double) throughout.
- The quotation mark should always be inside punctuation. (Except when the quotation is a complete sentence, when the fullstop is within the closing quotation mark.)

Reference citation in the text should be as brief as possible while directing the reader to the correct reference in the list of Works Cited. Footnotes should be kept to an absolute minimum. NEVER cite bibliographical information from memory; verify each entry carefully in your bibliography against the original source; and NEVER insert quotations from memory, always check against the text. We must rely on our contributors to be accurate in their citations. Here are some examples of how to list Works Cited:

BOOK BY SINGLE AUTHOR
Kipling, Rudyard. *Kim*. 1901. New York: Penguin Classics, 1987.

ANTHOLOGY or COMPILATION
Lopate, Phillip, ed. *The Art of the Personal Essay: An Anthology from the Classical Era to the Present*. New York: Anchor-Doubleday, 1994.

AN ARTICLE IN A JOURNAL WITH CONTINUOUS PAGINATION
Hanks, Patrick. 'Do Word Meanings Exist?' *Computers and the Humanities* 34 (2000): 205–15.

BASIC ENTRY DOCUMENT FROM INTERNET SITE
Zeki, Semir. 'Artistic Creativity and the Brain'. *Science* 6 July 2001: 51–52. *Science Magazine*. 2002. Amer. Assn. For the Advancement of Science. 24 Sept. 2002 < http://www.sciencemag.org/cgi/content/full/293/5527/51 > .

A full style sheet, including how to reference within the text, can be found on our website at www.wasafiri.org or will be sent out when a piece has been accepted.

**Early Electronic Offprints.** Corresponding authors can receive their article by email as a complete PDF file. This allows the author to print up to 50 copies, free of charge, and disseminate them to colleagues. Alternatively, corresponding authors can choose to receive the traditional 50 offprints. A copy of the journal will be sent by post to all corresponding authors after publication.

**Copyright.** It is a condition of publication that authors assign copyright or licence the publication rights in their articles to *Wasafiri*. This enables us to ensure full copyright protection and to disseminate the article, and of course the journal, to the widest possible readership in print and electronic formats as appropriate. Authors may, of course, use the article elsewhere *after* publication without prior permission provided that full acknowledgement is given to *Wasafiri* as the original source of publication, and that *Wasafiri*/Taylor & Francis are notified so that the records show that its use is properly authorised. Authors retain a number of other rights under the copyright and licensing policy documents. These policies are referred to at http://www.tandf.co.uk/journals/authorrights.pdf for full details. Authors are themselves responsible for obtaining permission to reproduce copyright material from other sources.

## Subscription Information

Wasafiri is a peer-reviewed journal published three times a year (March, July and November), by Routledge Journals, an imprint of Taylor & Francis, 4 Park Square, Milton Park, Abingdon, Oxfordshire OX14 4RN, UK.

### Annual Subscription, Volume 22, 2007 (Print ISSN 0269-0055)

Institutional   US$226   £129

Individual   US$50   £29

Online only   US$214   £122 (plus tax where applicable)

An institutional subscription to the print edition includes free access for any number of concurrent users across a local area network to the online edition, ISSN 1747-1508.
For more information, visit our website: http://www.tandf.co.uk/journals
For a complete and up-to-date guide to Taylor & Francis journals and books publishing programmes, and details of advertising in our journals, visit our website:
http://www.tandf.co.uk/journals

Dollar rates apply to subscribers in all countries except the UK and the Republic of Ireland where the pound sterling price applies. All subscriptions are payable in advance and all rates include postage. Journals are sent by air to the USA, Canada, Mexico, India, Japan and Australasia. Subscriptions are entered on an annual basis, i.e. January to December. Payment may be made by sterling cheque, dollar cheque, international money order, National Giro, or credit card (Amex, Visa, Mastercard).

### Ordering Information

**USA/Canada:** Taylor & Francis Inc., Journals Department, 325 Chestnut Street, 8th Floor, Philadelphia, PA 19106, USA. Tel: +1 (800) 354 1420; Fax: +1 (215) 625 8914. **Europe/Rest of World:** T&F Customer Services, T&F Informa UK Ltd, Sheepen Place, Colchester, Essex CO3 3LP, UK. Tel: +44 (o)207 017 5544; Fax: +44 (o)207 017 5198; Email: tf.enquiries@tfinforma.com

### Advertising Enquiries

**USA/Canada:** The Advertising Manager, Taylor & Francis Inc., 325 Chestnut Street, 8th Floor, Philadelphia, PA 19106, USA. Tel: +1 (215) 625 8900; Fax: +1 (215) 625 2240. **EU/RoW:** The Advertising Manager, Taylor & Francis, 4 Park Square, Milton Park, Abingdon, Oxfordshire OX14 4RN, UK. Tel: +44 (0) 207 017 6000. Fax: +44 (0) 207 017 6336.

### Back Issues

Taylor & Francis retains a three year back issue stock of journals. Older volumes are held by our official stockists: Periodicals Service Company, 11 Main Street, Germantown, NY 12526, USA to whom all orders and enquiries should be addressed. Telephone: +1 518 537 4700; Fax: +1 518 537 5899; E-mail: psc@periodicals.com

The print edition of this journal is typeset by Datapage, Dublin, Ireland and printed on ANSI conforming acid free paper by Hobbs The Printers, Hampshire, UK. The online edition of this journal is hosted by MetaPress at http://www.journalsonline.tandf.co.uk